Internationalizing the University

Also available from Continuum

Pedagogy and the University, Monica McLean
Perspectives of Quality in Adult Learning, Peter Boshier

Internationalizing the University

Yvonne Turner and Sue Robson

continuum

Continuum International Publishing Group

The Tower Building   80 Maiden Lane, Suite 704
11 York Road   New York, NY 10038
London
SE1 7NX

www.continuumbooks.com

British Library Cataloguing-in-Publication Data
A catalogue record for this book is available from the British Library.

ISBN: 9780826497833 (hardcover)

Library of Congress Cataloging-in-Publication Data

Turner, Yvonne.
    Internationalizing the university / Yvonne Turner & Sue Robson.
        p. cm.
    Includes bibliographical references and index.
    ISBN-13: 978-0-8264-9783-3 (hardcover)
    ISBN-10: 0-8264-9783-7 (hardcover)
    1. International education. 2. Education, Higher--International cooperation. 3. Globalization. I. Robson, Sue, MA. II. Title.

    LC1099.T87 2008
    378'.016--dc22

2007030487

Typeset by Free Range Book Design & Production Limited
Printed and bound in Great Britain by Biddles Ltd, King's Lynn, Norfolk

Contents

Introduction: the scope of the book

Globalization is changing the face of Higher Education (HE) across the world. Academics and students today are internationally mobile and unprecedented numbers of international exchanges, collaborations and cross-border education projects are springing up. The implications for individual Higher Education Institutions (HEIs) are significant. International students can bring much-needed revenues to boost institutional coffers and stimulate university classrooms but also have high expectations and demands. Academics and teachers face more opportunities for overseas work and collaboration as well as the challenges brought about by classroom diversity. University policy-makers confront a dynamic and unpredictable planning and management environment as they strive to meet the challenges of existing institutional commitments while steering institutions towards an ever-increasingly internationally integrated future. Everyone within HEI communities is touched in some way by international engagement and more and more of those people have explicit and direct responsibilities for the support or delivery of some aspect of internationalization, whether as a teacher, manager or service provider.

In spite of the widespread involvement in international matters in HEIs, there are relatively few practical resources available to help this growing community of people make sense of the phenomenon of internationalization and to guide and support the achievement of their responsibilities. Considerable literature has sprung up in recent years making a critical account of internationalization, linked to practice-based resources discussing the concerns and experiences of cross-border 'international' students in local classrooms. At the same time, little to date has focused on the broad practical issues confronting academic managers, education developers or others directly involved in day-to-day international work in HEIs and few accounts have presented internationalization as an integrated phenomenon affecting every aspect of life in the university community. This book aims, therefore, to provide a short introduction to the practical aspects of HE internationalization and to discuss its implications for those involved in managing the organizational processes that accompany it either as university managers or as teachers designing programmes and supporting the student experience. At the same time, this is not a 'how to' guide – internationalization is far too complex and dynamic a phenomenon to make any attempt at that kind of text either possible or useful. Instead, however, it is intended to provide a practically focused discussion of some of the key organizational issues confronting people in HE and to act as a stimulus to the discussions already taking place within universities. Moreover, the book arises directly out of our own experiences as academics and academic managers who continue to work in an internationalizing HE environment and whose work is international in scope and focus. A key concern in the text, therefore, is the need for HEIs, particularly in Anglophone countries, to evolve as part of an internationally integrated community rather than continue as historically constituted national institutions which work simply to accommodate the needs of people from other countries into their pre-existing practices. The emphasis throughout the discussion is on the development of inter-cultural awareness for university people supported by sustainable international management practices.

The book addresses a number of practical themes, beginning with a short discussion about globalization and internationalization in Chapter 1. In Chapters 2 and 3 the discussion focuses down on the characteristics of an international HEI and explores the more tangible elements of internationalization at an institutional level, especially those that govern assumptions about educational practices. Chapters 4 to 6 address some of the educational challenges attaching to internationalizing academic practices and supporting student learning in a culturally inclusive educational environment. Chapters 7 and 8 address the specific management and academic development issues that emerge out of the discussion in the preceding chapters. Throughout the text the emphasis is on practical action and collaborative decision-making, highlighting the socially mediated nature of internationalization and long-term sustainability of international initiatives undertaken within HEIs.

Notwithstanding the practical focus of the book outlined above, it is essential to begin with a brief orientation to the main features in the landscape we will be charting: HE globalization and internationalization. We begin in Chapter 1 with a brief overview of the impact of HE globalization and discuss the resonances between internationalization and globalization phenomena. The chapter concludes with a more detailed assessment of the conceptual dimensions of HE internationalization.

Chapter 1

The globalization of higher education: concepts and context

Finding a compass: HE globalization and international engagement

Discussions about HE globalization have been a long-term feature in educational discourse, over more than 20 years. Inevitably such discussions have related strongly to commentaries about the nature of economic globalization which have featured across disciplines and become a matter of reporting cliché. The territory of globalization, however, and in particular its impact on local institutional practices, still remains contested. Indeed, beyond the terms of implying a simple increase in international traffic, the existence of globalization and the nature of its impact, the influence of local context and the likely outcomes of globalization processes remain unclear within the discourse.

Plainly at its broadest level globalization relates to the increasing interconnectedness of communication and influence around the world. Its impacts are identified most strongly with the communication, technology and economic spheres, therefore. A broad consensus now exists that, within economic and trade systems, the linkages between information and communications technologies and increases in the volumes of international trade have wrought significant changes on individual nation states and on regional and international institutions. Within education, globalization is often allied to or given responsibility for initiating changes in the style and shape of educational institutions. This is seen mainly thorough its stimulus to movements such as 'Academic Capitalism' (Slaughter and Leslie, 1997), 'Enterprise Universities' (Schapper and Mayson, 2004; Edwards *et al.*, 2003) and changes in national government policies and funding stances towards the HE sector around the world. Globalization is usually regarded as responsible for dramatically increasing cross-border student and academic mobility, as national borders have opened up and global trade has had a significant impact on local economies, driving increasing demand for HE and English language education, particularly in applied subjects such as business and education studies. Resonances from the globalization phenomenon are also to be found in increasing interest in issues such as 'knowledge-transfer' and 'knowledge-sharing' as cross-border research collaborations and international commercial applications of HE research developments grow in number and diversity (Altbach, 1989a, b; MacKinnon, 1998; Hanna and Latchem, 2002). Ultimately, globalization is regarded as responsible for the emergence of new forms of HE provision, in the explosion of distance learning programmes intended for international participation and the development of transnational and other cross-border educational partnerships and collaborations (Heyneman, 2001; Hanna and Latchem, 2002; Rouhani and Kishun, 2004).

In a general sense, therefore, the notion of globalization in HE seems to relate to a growing porosity between historically national institutions and an increasingly internationally integrated educational world. The processes of globalization are challenging local cultural assumptions and eroding or reshaping ideas about educational practices in the light of increasing international contact (Astiz, Wiseman and Baker, 2002). At the same time, however, some commentators are challenging the 'strong globalization' metaphor, especially in its application to education (Matthews, 2002; Angus, 2004; Dixon, 2006). Other researchers identify parallel changes taking place in HE rather than attributing globalization as the root cause of the undoubted shifts taking place across the sector (Deem, 2001; Carnoy and Rhoten, 2002). Many ascribe significant impacts arising from local context that change the face of globalization, producing diverse, counterintuitive effects which strongly contradict the dominant rhetoric of globalization (Clayton, 2004; Ensor, 2004).

Ultimately a lack of consensus remains between those who see globalization as a strong or weak force acting upon HE; between divergence and convergence; between causality and simultaneity; between the eroding influence of local/national cultures in the face of the emergence of a new 'global' culture and the re-emergence of individuated local differentiation in the face of increasing diversity. What remains clear, is that a significant volume of HE discourse, in both theoretical and practice-based commentaries responds in some way to the broader discourse of globalization in its various guises. Inevitably, however, the lack of consensus about globalization has an impact on the language employed in discussing the phenomenon. Such ambivalence also leaches into considerations of the related concept of HE Internationalization.

HE internationalization: problematic definitions

In parallel to globalization, many accounts of internationalization also depict national HE as increasingly defined by supranational concerns. Regarded as a channel for educational opening-up and knowledge-exchange (Bennell and Pearce, 2003), as a stimulus for international marketing opportunities (De Vita and Case, 2003), a prompt for international research collaboration (Teichler, 2004) or as a descriptor of cross-border student flows (Huang, 1997; Humfrey, 1999), the language of internationalization has been captured within a number of different educational discourses. Discussions about internationalization have also figured alongside globalization in the discourse of the commercialization of HE and the emergence of university entrepreneurship (Hanna and Latchem, 2002; Feast and Bretag, 2005). As such, the increasing cross-border traffic implied by internationalization has been characterized as both an energizing catalyst for international knowledge-sharing and a negative neo-liberal ideological force, transporting the worst of corporate managerialism into academic life. Partly because of the pervasiveness of internationalization as a theme within the contemporary discourse as well as its ideological resonances, however, it remains difficult to pin down the concept and relate it to practical phenomena within the routine experiences of people in HEIs. The high-level nature of many attempts at definition compound this difficulty. Here is a well-established characterization:

> Internationalization at the national, sector and institutional levels is defined as the process of integrating an international, intercultural or global dimension into the purpose, functions or delivery of postsecondary education. (Knight, J., 2003, p. 2)

While providing a useful way of generally conceiving of internationalization and providing focus for debate, more detailed definitions are often unsatisfactory, however, and relate only in the broadest sense to what people in universities do while they are at work every day. The majority of accounts to date have focused discussions on theoretical, policy and market areas or have explored the experiences of international students rather than the more varied concerns of academics and managers. Yet if international engagement is to be enlivened and understood, translated into institutional policy and practices, then a clear practical framework to underpin work in the area of internationalization seems necessary.

Globalization and internationalization: mapping the international territory

The preceding brief discussion suggests that globalization and internationalization discourses relate very strongly to each other, in the broad concerns which they highlight and in the degree to which both concepts are contested (deWit, 2002; Knight, 2004). Certainly the terms are ubiquitous in the HE literature. Ultimately both stand as sense-making metaphors, commonly employed to account for the increasing international connectedness and mobility that is evident within HEIs in many countries. In a general sense, the parallel notions identify a number of common implications for institutional structures and practices, including:

- Increasing organizational and management complexity as HEIs need to operate in multiple physical and technological environments.
- The development of a distributed knowledge-production system, encouraging the proliferation of international public and private sector educational and knowledge-production organizations which are challenging the historic supremacy of universities.
- Increasing student and employee diversity, linked to diverse locations and modes of involvement with HEIs.
- Challenges to locally valid educational and intellectual customs and practices in the face of cultural diversity.
- The requirement to reconcile potentially conflicting education-as-trade and educational-as-knowledge-sharing efforts operationally and strategically.

Notwithstanding these elements of commonality, however, the notions of globalization and internationalization also carry distinctively different resonances and stand in dialectical relationship to each other (Scott, 1998; Van der Wende, 2001; Matthews, 2002; Gacel-Avila, 2005). It is useful, therefore, to get a sense of the nature of these distinctions in order to clarify why a focus on internationalization is, in our view, a more appropriate conceptual response to considering international engagement than the parallel notion of globalization.

The first and most obvious distinction between them lies in the notion of nationality and the treatment of national boundaries. In the mainstream discourse of globalization, increasing international contact is generally regarded as eroding national boundaries and redefining the relationship between citizenship, consumption and mobility (Deem, 2001; Held *et al.*, 1999). Green's (1997) notion of the developmental state marks a mid-point in the range of positions most commonly adopted in respect of the power of the nation state in respect to education. In this model, deregulation and small government facilitates increasing HE autonomy and asserts the role of the market in shaping the development of HE sectors. Globalization is, therefore, regarded as prompting increasing commercialization within HE and the historic national character of individual institutions and distinctiveness between national systems is reduced through global convergence encouraged by market forces (McWilliam et al., 1999; Morey, 2004). On the other hand, the discourse of internationalization tends to reassert the continued role of national boundaries and national distinctiveness both at sectoral and institutional levels. International engagement takes the form of cooperation and focuses on bridging differences in a context that is simultaneously convergent and divergent rather than suggesting straightforward movement towards the demands of the market (Rouhani and Kishun, 2004). This analysis also tends to assert the continued presence of national policy frameworks as an important influence on the shape of HE rather than minimizing their relevance. As a consequence, internationalization discourse tempers the dominance of the free market as a determinant of HE activity. In this construction, national policy priorities and local context work as forces together with and are not entirely subordinated to the linear pull of the market. Clearly, then, one key differentiation between globalization and internationalization in terms of boundaries lies in the dominant underlying metaphor of HE as either a national civic institution or as a predominantly market entity governed by the dynamics of global consumer demand.

Within the general differentiation outlined above, interesting variances emerge when considering the directional impetus in discussions drawing on globalization or internationalization as a framework for analysis. Clearly within the globalization literature considerable impetus is given to convergence theories, allied to the decline of national identity and control and the convergence of service offerings to meet the demands of globally mobile consumers (Clayton, 2004; Ortiz, 2004). The focus in the internationalization discourse on national distinctiveness indicates a more divergent approach stemming from the array of local cultures and practices around the world. Linked to this in the HE literature, however, is a sense that globalization stems from a wide diversity of different inputs that are marshalled externally to HE and individual HEIs and which are bearing external forces into organizations. On the other hand, within the discourse of internationalization there is an underlying notion that, though external globalizing forces certainly exist, the support of local context, national policy frameworks and pre-existing institutional practices endow HEIs with a wider range of choices about how to respond (Kawaguchi and Lander, 1997; Gillespie, 2002; Matthews, 2002). This also implies that convergence on market demands may not be the inevitable or only possibility. To some extent, therefore, what is captured by the discourse of internationalization is a broader range of opportunities – hence more divergence – than seems possible within much of the thrust behind the HE globalization literature. Even where that is not the case, discussions about internationalization are often framed within a practice-based assessment of changes taking place within institutions rather than relating directly to higher level theoretical stances. Internationalization, therefore, tends to describe what might be called 'push' strategies as institutions seek out intercultural opportunities, sometimes acknowledging globalizing trends and sometimes unconscious of them. The globalization literature, on the other hand, frequently focuses on 'pull' strategies as institutional actions are causally ascribed to broader, external trends and interpreted as within a conscious context of wider movements within world societies.

In spite of these differences, however, it remains clear that the language of globalization and internationalization map similar territory in many of the HE commentaries. Some researchers regard internationalization as an accompaniment of globalization and others ascribe them as alternatives or in opposition to each other (Yang, 2002; Vaira, 2004). The volume of the literature provides plenty of opportunities to adopt either metaphor to justify and describe any particular position. The context of this book, however, lies very much within the realms of current practice – the main focus of the internationalization literature – and, as much for the sake of simplicity as anything else, therefore, we have adopted the language of internationalization in our assessment of contemporary HE changes. Nonetheless this adoption of the language of internationalization also encompasses some particular values and beliefs which actively diverge from the discourse of globalization as well as a simple measure of convenience.

Internationalization, ideology and contemporary practices

Problematically, the term globalization has become tainted both by its ubiquity as well as elements of its ideology (Bradley *et al.*, 2000). Assertions about the decline of national identity and power and the overwhelming dominance of the market as a force identified in much of the globalization literature is something which impacts at different levels in different places and about which both institutions and nation states may still have some choices (Woolf, 2002). For this reason, the softer term internationalization seems more appropriate in discussing the phenomena in which we are interested, partly because most HEIs do not at this time exist as fully marketized entities and many function within quasi public-private contexts with multiple disparate sources of income and control. The concept of internationalization, therefore, seems to be effectively based in the contemporary realities that confront HEIs and academic managers in their day-to-day work. Secondly, internationalization relates closely to the operational decisions that people in individual institutions choose to make. The term lends considerable scope and flexibility in determining how much and what style of international engagement might be possible or desirable in any particular place and time. Thirdly, internationalization as a set of values resonates with long-standing notions of internationalism and reciprocity – a respect for continued cultural and intellectual diversity – whereas aspects of the globalization debate assert such strong positive aspirations towards the development of 'global culture' that the contribution of diversity seems undervalued (Dixon, 2006). Globalization also remains conceptually and intellectually unresolved. The lack of consensus and uncertainty around this particular metaphor is such that it becomes difficult to work clearly in its context when discussing operational practices and organizational planning and development. Internationalization seems both more accessible and appropriate, either as a stepping-stone to yet unrealized globalization or as a more accessible and practicable choice of metaphor for action.

For all the uncertainties about the scope and shape of internationalization, its relationship to globalization and the labile composition of the basic concepts, the literature shows a fairly clear consensus about the depth of the impact on HE and the breadth of its consequences for 'policy-making, governance and academic work and identity' (Vaira, 2004, p. 489). It is important, therefore, to consider the implications of the style of response to international engagement inherent in the debate. For many practice-focused commentators, there is an increasing tendency to regard the impact of internationalization as a universal or unitarist phenomenon (Angus, 2004). Others, however, especially those researching outside of the dominant Anglo-European educational context or adopting a post-colonial perspective, for example, regard internationalization as a phenomenon further complicated by its very different constitution in different places (Rizvi, Lingard and Lavia, 2006). Some contrast globalization and internationalization – the former primarily about economic processes and the latter about engagement and knowledge-sharing – but also associate internationalization as articulated in rapidly developing countries such as China with the processes of the intellectual 'Westernization' (Gibbons, 1998; Yang 2001, 2002; Matthews, 2002). Others also assert the importance of local context in shaping the idiosyncrasies of local responses to broadly globalizing phenomena in education and critique a blanket reliance on the universalist language of globalization to account for the range of changes taking place in contemporary education (Deem 2001; Crabtree and Sapp, 2004; Mok, 2005; Rochford, 2006). Such discourse is inevitably compounded by the ideological aspects of much of the discussion that accompanies many assessments of educational globalization. It is clear that, if educational globalization is taking place, then we are witnessing what are its earliest manifestations and that the implications of much of what is happening are as yet unclear. What emerges from such analyses, therefore, is a sense that contrasting internationalization as somehow the 'good guy' to globalization's 'bad guy' is overly simplistic. Rather internationalization should most properly be regarded as one attempt to capture the highly complex and contradictory processes attaching to the increasing international traffic that is occurring between nationally based HE institutions and knowledge systems, which does not necessarily provide insight into the specific styles or character of response that will shape internationalization in particular local environments.

Internationalization and inclusivity

The preceding discussion highlights a key contradiction when adopting an orientation towards internationalization over globalization. On the one hand, this text is positioned within the context of internationalization and international inclusivity. At the same time, the inevitable issue of the treatment of 'Cultural Others' within local education contexts intrudes into that orientation. If one accepts the reality of diverse academic practices and values in different settings, then issues of cultural insider and outsider participants in local education become problematic. The rhetoric of globalization appears to provide simple solutions to this difficulty by offering the seductive possibility of the evolution of a hybrid global culture which would enable everyone to participate as insiders wherever they happen to be working or studying and wherever they come from (Held *et al.*, 1999). Such a notion is unsatisfactory, however, because it underplays the challenges of unequal influence in the evolution of global culture (Scott, 1998; Teichler, 2004; Gacel-Avila, 2005). The concerns of post-colonial researchers throw this difficulty into strong relief, underlined by more general critiques of cultural 'Westernization' implied by globalizing tendencies in business and economic globalization (Devos, 2003; Rasool, 2004). In educational terms, however, the spread of 'Western' education practices and beliefs – sometimes adopted as a synonym for 'global' – clearly cannot imply a truly equal or negotiated intellectual space (AUT/DEA, 1999). Ultimately the rhetoric of educational globalization may well obscure rather than highlight very important geo-political issues of power and influence (Kogan, 2005). This is particularly the case with contemporary university education, given its historical roots as essentially a European institution, introduced to many countries around the world as a direct result of political imperialism (Scott, 1995; Mayor, 1998; deWit, 2002).

Contrasting the shrouding of unequal power distribution inherent in much of the discourse of globalization, the context of 'internationalization' brings the diversity of local, national and regional cultures explicitly to the fore as a key focus for debate. Internationalization, therefore, forces consideration of extremely important issues about who shapes the culture of learning and intellectual HE spaces and who determines the norms of discourse within academic communities. It is because of its very focus on local cultural practices that the language of internationalization encourages explicit debate and active decision-making about values, culturally problematizing HE practices in the face of international diversity. The concept of internationalization is itself dialectical therefore. A focus on internationalization does not assert an unchallenged dominance of the local over cultural others, nor does it posit national educational practices as somehow incommensurable. Instead, however, internationalization discourse is inherently dialogic, providing both an intellectual and a practical space in which to identify, discuss and bridge differences in the context of celebrating diversity rather than seeking to eradicate it.

Operational internationalization: a conceptual approach

As we discussed above, at its broadest level, internationalization acts as a metaphor which describes increasing international engagement within universities. The key difficulty with this definition of internationalization lies in its conceptual and theoretical lack of precision. This is particularly the case because internationalization is a multi-stranded concept embracing the motivation and spirit in which international engagement is undertaken as much as describing tangible organizational activities (Devos, 2003; Carroll and Ryan, 2005). For university managers in particular, this presents a range of strategic and operational challenges. If internationalization exists as such a different phenomenon in different contexts, how is it possible to understand an individual institution's orientation to it, let alone manage organizational progress towards a desired style or level of engagement? To counter these valid concerns, there are, however, some generic themes that repeat within the discourse of internationalization and can provide access to a conceptual understanding of it. These themes are summarized at Figure 1.1.

Figure 1.1: Multi-dimensional internationalization

Theme	Definition	Dimensions
1. International engagement	International contact and activity	National and institutional policy, partnerships, strategic orientation and extent of institution's strategic commitment to international activities; mix of internationalization abroad and internationalization at home
2. Mobility	Flows of students, academics, employees into and out of institution	International student recruitment; international educational partnerships; international staff employment; academic exchanges, international career development for institutional employees; student exchanges, placements, etc.
3. Revenues	Revenue generation from/revenue expenditure on international development and activities	International student fee income; research projects; international knowledge exports/imports; international third strand/ commercial income

Figure 1.1 continued

Theme	Definition	Dimensions
4. **International professionals**	Staff with specific responsibility for international matters	International offices; professional recruiters, marketers and/or managers and administrators with designated executive responsibility for international matters; use of expatriate staff to support international engagement
5. **Communication**	Communication systems/communication outputs focused on international matters	Websites, recruitment materials, research information, management information production; media information and public relations.
6. **Knowledge-sharing**	Research and partnerships; international business spin-offs, intellectual property/patents, etc.	Institutional leadership in international research; applied international joint-venture activities; cultural style and orientation of engagement
7. **Language**	Language policy and practice matters	Institutional languages in use/language diversity (formally adopted and informal); languages employed in teaching programmes; language teaching volume and organization; English language programming/'local-language-as-a-foreign-language' provision
8. **Programming and curriculum**	Shifts in programming, style, content, range, point and mode of delivery; international coverage within teaching content	Development of 'international' programmes; transnational projects; new / bespoke programming for international participation; convergence on international programme types, e.g. Bachelor's, Master's and Doctoral models for degree programmes; degree of disciplinary ethnocentrism within teaching curriculum; source of learning materials and resources; redesign of curriculum to take account of international participation

Figure 1.1 continued

Theme	Definition	Dimensions
9. Academic practices	Cultural pedagogy, teaching and learning practices, diversity and inclusivity	Local teaching and learning practices vs. convergence on 'international'/'Western' model; unitarist vs. pluralist teaching practices; extent and role of local civic education; academic development to support international inclusivity
10. Reciprocity/ 'Westernization'	Basic philosophical orientation to internationalization	Uni-directional/universal vs. multi-directional/pluralist flow within the above nine themes; degree of emphasis on international collaboration and equality of partnerships; ethnocentric vs. ethnorelative values reflected in institutional policies and practices; transparency of values in institutional policy and practices

The presence of each dimension on the list indicates that it has featured in a range of discussions within the internationalization literature. The list is not exclusive or synergistic, however. Certainly orientations towards the themes and issues indicated vary considerably in both empirical, practice-based cases reported in the literature and in the various theoretical debates. Taken as a whole, however, the list provides a useful set of dimensional boundaries for any conceptual discussion of internationalization and can function as a preliminary diagnostic for assessing the volume of international activity within an institution.

Exploring the dimensions

Within the overall schema in Figure 1.1 the list of factors represents a broad typology characterizing internationalization and moving from general, sectoral dimensions through increasing detail into institutional and managerial issues towards practice and pedagogical matters. As noted above, each of the dimensions are reflected within the wide spectrum of practice-based, managerial and critical literature that addresses internationalization. The handling and focus of the discourse within each of these areas occupies a wide variety, however, and is often contradictory. At the most general level, therefore, this list of issues provides an opportunity for institutions to explore the broad state and style of their internationalization at any one point in time. In doing so it is important to emphasize the extent of variability in the debates present within individual aspects of the list and to regard this set of dimensions as descriptive and exploratory rather than providing a simple tool for an activity-based assessment of international engagement. Implicitly embedded within the list of factors are important qualitative discussions about international orientation and style as well as simple indicators of volumes of activities which we will discuss in Chapters 2 and 3.

1. International engagement

The first dimension is relatively straightforward and is perhaps the most basic attribute of internationalization. At its most general, internationalization simply relates to the volume and style of international traffic that flows across national or institutional boundaries and the literature reflects that, particularly breaking down into two broad emphases: Internationalization Abroad (international HE as a national export) and Internationalization at Home (the embedding of international/intercultural perspectives into local educational settings). This dimension, therefore, encompasses a wide range of aspects of international activity at policy, managerial and practice levels. Within this dimension, it is also useful to consider the chronology and the extent to which policy frameworks are prospective or retrospective in nature. In the UK, for example, both government and institutional policies in recent years have anticipated levels of actual international engagement and have sought more to stimulate and organize nascent internationalization in UK HE rather than respond to significant levels of pre-existing internationalization across the sector (Ottewill and MacFarlane, 2003; Hatakenaka, 2004). This dimension also indicates the general emphasis of internationalization within any context, whether it is political in nature or aimed at educational exchange, whether the thrust is economic and focused on revenue generation or about international aid and knowledge-sharing.

2. Mobility

This dimension also looms large within any evaluation of internationalization. It is often one of the primary prompts in determining whether internationalization is taking place and is indicated as a key internationalizing factor within most of the literature. Again there are interesting patterns within this dimension, indicating particularly whether international mobility is a phenomenon that affects primarily academic workers or students and is constructed as an inward, outward or reciprocal flow. In this area, some of the sharpest divisions arise between commentators from primarily marketized Anglophone nations and those from newly emerging economies or within post-colonial contexts (Tremblay, 2005). Thus orientations towards mobility are variously regarded as problems of brain drain, bringing knowledge and education-based tensions to a national context or are constructed as economically useful, with international students and academics providing knowledge and financial inputs to local HE sectors (Kishun, 1998; Yan, 1998; Andere, 2004; Bekhradnia and Sastry, 2005; Postiglione, 2005).

3. Revenues

Following on from point 2 above, the issue of revenues is a key dimension within discussions of internationalization and represents one of the major elisions within the internationalization and globalization discourses. The economic valuing of knowledge and education-based internationalization resonates across a range of areas. The focus within the majority of the literature lies in discussions about student fee revenue and the commercialization of HE across the world, with several strands focusing on the commercial benefits of English language medium educational programming (see point 7). The nature of the revenue flows and the importance given to revenue over other cultural and social considerations, however, also acts as a useful indicator of institutional and national dynamics and general orientation within international matters. The discourse shows a wide range of orientations to discussions of the revenue elements within an assessment of internationalization. For some, revenue is a primary driver in internationalizing efforts while others make a critique of competitive approaches to internationalization through revenue generation or strand the discussion between those institutions/ nations who are more or less market-based (Luijten-Lub *et al.*, 2005; Asteris, 2006). This is largely dependant on the corresponding view of the relationship between internationalization and globalization. On the whole, however, revenues feature strongly in the majority of discussions and are certainly employed as a key indicator that internationalization is taking place.

4. International professionals

This dimension reflects quite specific elements within the discourse which often stand outside much of the main academic HE internationalization literature. Nonetheless it is clear that the presence of professionals at institutional level with a specific brief for international matters, whether as recruiters of students within formally constituted international offices or institutional policy-makers, remains a broad indicator of international activity and also reflects the style and approach to internationalization within a particular environment. Much of the literature that focuses on this area responds to the competitive and recruitment-focused activities of international offices. It is frequently produced by governmental or national organizations such as IDP Australia and the British Council or special interest groups such as UKCISA (UK Council for International Student Affairs) and ICOS (Irish Council for Overseas Students). The style of discourse in this dimension is different therefore and often addresses itself directly to a management or operational audience rather than to an academic one. The presence of international professionals within the institutional infrastructure and the specific nature of their responsibilities, however, remain a useful indicator of overall international orientation. Equally the literature dealing with international matters from outside the academic critical canon also remains important.

5. Communication

Information and communication technologies (ICTs), communication systems and the aims and purposes of communication are a clear indicator of the extent of international traffic. The internationalizing potential of ICTs is well covered in the literature, especially when considering technologically mediated programming within an educational context (Farquhar, 1999; Ciges, 2001; Duke, 2002; Thune and Welle-Strand, 2005). Equally, issues of poor communication and critiques of the style and approach of communication both between institutions and prospective international students and within institutions remains an important sub-text within much of the broader internationalization discourse (Cortazzi and Jin, 1997; Mortimer, 1997; Ryan, 2000; Major, 2005; Turner, 2006a).

6. Knowledge-sharing

Within the general internationalization literature, knowledge-sharing has featured rather less than discussions about academic practice and management or organization issues. Within a wider spectrum, however, debates about the nature of knowledge-sharing or knowledge-transfer bring significant implications to any discussion of HE internationalization (Middlehurst and Woodfield, 2007; Weert, 2006). Certainly in terms of flows and styles of activities, knowledge-sharing orientations and volumes of traffic make an important contribution. In a general sense, however, much of the discussion about the international commercialization of knowledge, knowledge imports and exports and their economic and social consequences remain within specific fields related to but not necessarily within the canon of internationalization literature.

7. Language

The discourse in this area reflects growth of English language medium teaching programmes in many countries around the world and is articulated in many academic practice and teaching and learning commentaries, exploring the language implications for cross-border second-language learners as well as for providers (Pennycook, 1994, 1998; Newman *et al.*, 2003; Zhu, 2004; Luijten-Lub, Van der Wende, Huisman, 2005). The literature also discusses the implications of the extensive recruitment of English language speakers on university staffs, and growth of English-as-a-foreign-language/local-language-as-a-foreign-language teaching and testing provision around the world (Yang, 2001; Bennell and Pearce, 2003). Some of the literature also focuses on issues concerned with the status of local languages in, for example, teaching and academic publication and language policies adopted within a particular environmental setting (Yang, 2001, 2002).

8. Programming and curriculum

Programming and curriculum issues have received considerable attention in the internationalization of teaching and learning literature.

Shifts in programming towards, for example, commercial models, accelerated progression programmes, vocational subjects of study and the general emergence of short-duration taught postgraduate degrees lie beside discussions addressing global and regional policy issues such as the Bologna process within Europe, for example (Chaabane and Mouss, 1998; Paterson, 2001; Hanna and Latchem, 2002). Both at a practical level and within the discourse, therefore, styles of programming and delivery issues more generally remain a very important indicator of international effort and emphasis both at institutional and at sectoral levels (Welch, 2002). Discourse about internationalization of the curriculum highlights discussions mainly at design level, though some literature exists within the disciplines, which discusses cultural issues within curriculum content and delivery.

9. Academic practices

The past ten years has seen an explosion of academic practice literature, particularly from within Anglophone countries, in response to increasing student international diversity. It is broad in its context and the style of its discussion about the issues. Nonetheless academic practice issues remain a key dimension of internationalization throughout the literature (Barker, 1997; Macrae, 1997; Leask, 2001; Samuelowicz and Bain, 2001; Devos, 2003; Johnson and Deem, 2003). Again great variety exists in the style and focus of discussions. Practice expositions exist in great numbers which endorse a variety of approaches to managing cohort or student diversity while others critique implicit or local models of practice and evaluate particular curriculum issues (Cassidy and Eachus, 2000; De Vita, 2002; Butcher and McGrath, 2004; Camiciotolli, 2005). Therefore, the literature is as much practical as it is discourse-based. The relationship between academic practice issues and internationalization seems as intimate as it is complex. A whole raft of stylistic and activity-based assessments emerge within this area for consideration and, again, the globalization debate emerges here, though often more implicitly and more subdued than within the commentaries that focus strongly on revenue effects or student recruitment. Overall, however, considerable attention must be given to academic practice and pedagogical issues within an assessment of internationalization.

10. Reciprocal internationalization

Underlying the other nine dimensions shown in Figure 1.1 perhaps the most fundamental, values-based aspect attaching to internationalization is that of international Reciprocity/ 'Westernization'. In many practice-based commentaries much of this discussion remains implicit, silently asserting a model of HE practice which is enculturated rather than culturally problematized. However, the implications of the tacit transfer of an enculturated pedagogy around the world features in an increasing number of commentaries which question the sustainability of some forms of international engagement and educational exchange, especially in Anglophone countries (Samuelowicz and Bain, 2001; Woodrow, 2001; Welch, 2002; Sanderson, 2004; Walker, 2004). To a large extent many of the other dimensions are relatively uncontentious and describe educational or organizational practices against which an institution might readily assess itself. Commentaries may differ in the advocated style or orientation taken to any particular theme but, within that, there remains a reasonable consensus that international engagement is captured in some way by all or some of the dimensions just discussed. In considering reciprocal internationalization, a greater variation emerges in the literature, however, especially between the managerial, practice-based literature and the HE globalization literature when discussing the nature of reciprocity. For those who focus largely on the economic benefits of HE globalization – the so-called Hyperglobalists (Held, McGrew, Goldblatt and Perraton, 1999) – and educational or epistemological absolutists who have focused on the cultural neutrality of scientific and academic practices, issues of convergence on particular intellectual or educational paradigms remain relatively uncontentious (Smith, 1998; Brown, 1998; Kumar and Usunier, 2001; Knight, 2002). Indeed the concept of knowledge-transfer makes extensive epistemological as well as technological assumptions about the nature of globalization-driven knowledge-sharing from so-called 'advanced' countries in the world to newly emerging economies. For post-colonial writers, and educational relativists, among others adopting a divergent position on the processes of HE globalization, however, the notion of reciprocity is foregrounded in discussions about internationalization and adds a strongly ideological dimension to its underlying character (Meek, 2000; Gillespie, 2002; Gacel-Avila, 2005). Here the emphasis conceptually as well as practically is on internationalization as a two-way or multi-directional flow of practices and influence. As such 'Westernization' (or the privileging of any particular local practices or values in an international setting) and 'reciprocity' are raised as antithetical in the list. We will discuss the practical organizational implications of these differences for institutional engagement further in Chapters 2 and 3. It remains clear, however, that in some way internationalization articulated as either a unidirectional or reciprocal flow of values and influence, practices, money and people emerges as a strong underlying theme in many of the other dimensions, binding together the other more practical elements and lending a particular style or orientation to engagement. Certainly the inclusion of reciprocity and discussions of Westernization bring strong social and political tones to any evaluation of internationalization. It is clearly in this area that the connections between internationalization and the broader debates attaching to HE globalization are foregrounded. The inclusion of reciprocity in the list of dimensions of internationalization, therefore, is an important binding element, and highlights the dynamic, contingent and discursive nature of the conceptual boundaries as a whole. As we will discuss in Chapter 2, the issue of reciprocity is also indicated as a key factor in the achievement of long-term sustainable internationalization.

Conclusion: working within the ten dimensions

Taken as a whole, the ten themes outlined in Figure 1.1 enable us to get a reasonably clear sense of what is broadly implied by internationalization and to gain an initial view of the complexity of its scope. It is also useful as a means of understanding both the linkages and the differentiation in emphasis between internationalization and globalization that have emerged from the foregoing discussion. It is clear that the reach of the ten dimensions into the institutional and academic psyche is profound, touching upon management and academic practices, pedagogies and educational policy-making as well as the personal values and beliefs of people within the HE community. In their articulation, the pervasive potential of internationalization for HE shows itself to be equally profound. Collectively the dimensions enable a preliminary qualitative assessment of the ways in which internationalization is influencing institutional activities and to establish a framework within which to consider priorities and contradictions within an overall stance towards internationalization. Indeed, the literature shows a reasonably strong consensus that programmes, students and academics are all central factors in increasing international engagement. It is also clear that revenue streams and the business focus of the institution are in some way important in the process. What is less clear from the literature, however, is the relative emphasis of the different elements within internationalization and the practical implications of managing towards a differing configuration. In effect, the list of dimensions functions as a map setting out the boundaries and key features of the internationalization territory. It is less useful as a tool for orienting around it or for helping to diagnose its topographical character. As we have discussed above, one of the main practical drawbacks within much of the literature to date is that omission. While discussions about concepts and teaching and learning practices have proliferated, an assessment of the institutional and management impacts is less evident. Drawing on the foundation laid out in this chapter, therefore, we will begin to draw out a more practical institutional framework in Chapter 2.

Chapter 2

An international institution

Introduction: from concepts to practices

Building on the wider conceptual discussions about internationalization and the globalization of HE highlighted in Chapter 1, this chapter goes on to explore some of the practical challenges associated with the phenomenon of internationalization at an institutional level. Broadly focused on aspects of the debate within the literature which indicate the rhetorical gap between cited and actual motivations for institutional internationalization, it explores the strategic impact of mass commercial internationalization upon the HE community. Populating the broad descriptions of the dimensions of internationalization outlined in Chapter 1, this chapter attempts to make a more coherent and evaluative assessment of the factors involved in internationalizing HEIs and to resolve some of the contradictions and wide differences that emerge within the discourse. It is also more directly focused on practical and institutional issues. We will discuss the operational management challenges inherent in internationalization in more detail in Chapter 7 but this chapter sets out to provide a framework in which institutions might characterize their level of international engagement and assess the ways in which they might wish to make a managed process of alignment to meet their policy aspirations and wider environmental dynamics.

Internationalization in specific contexts

As we have discussed, internationalization has impacted widely upon HE in the past two decades, reflecting the broad globalizing trends which at first prompted increases in academic mobility and stimulated demand for English language medium education, especially from countries such as China and India. DeWit (2002) identifies four generic rationales for internationalization within HE:

Political: responding to prompts from foreign policy, national security, technical assistance, peace and mutual understanding, national and regional identity.

Economic: responding to prompts from economic growth and competitiveness, the labour market, national educational demand, financial incentives for institutions and governments.

Cultural and social: the export of national culture, high culture and universalism, individual benefit/personal development, academic exchange, global awareness.

Academic: providing an international dimension to research and teaching, extending the academic horizon, institution-building, profile and status, quality enhancement, international academic standards.

Building on these general impulses to internationalization, historical development within particular contexts has also shifted its focus. In Europe, for example, internationalization developed in four phases during the late twentieth and early twenty-first centuries (Wachter, 2003). From the 1980s it was a marginal activity based on individual mobility, from the 1980s–90s institutions saw higher levels of international mobility with the development of departmental units of organizations within institutions. From the mid-1990s, the EU stimulated the development of curricular internationalization and the late 1990s, post-Bologna period saw responses to the world market in higher education and educational globalization together with a shift to Internationalization at Home.

As an early indicator of incipient internationalization, the presence of international students has had an impact on many aspects of university activities and identity. Overseas students studying in Britain, for example, have grown both in numbers and in the range of their countries of origin, broadening the cultural diversity of the university community (*Times Higher Education Supplement*, 2006c; UKCOSA, 2006). In common with the experience in a range of Anglophone countries, their participation has influenced programming and curriculum in specific ways, notably though the development of one-year taught postgraduate programmes in vocational subjects such as business and education studies (Sastry, 2004; Turner, 2002a, b; 2006a). In addition, British universities have also looked towards overseas students as a source of revenue in response to declining central grants as shifts in government policy restructured HE funding during the late twentieth century and encouraged universities to attempt to maximize the revenue contribution from premium fee-paying students, including those from overseas (Humfrey 1999; Hodges, 2001; De Vita and Case, 2003; Bekhradnia, 2006; HEPI, 2006).

Inevitably, internationalization brings with it broader organizational impacts than those immediately associated with the participation of more overseas students. For example, academic recruitment and retention issues have also had an impact on the international reach of employment patterns and organizational systems (Scott, 1998; Bekhradnia and Sastry, 2005). In addition, international knowledge-sharing and research efforts, especially in the natural sciences, have developed rapidly, supported by technological advances in information and communication sciences. As a result, universities in the UK and many Anglophone countries around the world are increasingly engaging in international collaborations and partnerships of varying kinds, including the establishment of transnational ventures (Doorbar, 2004; Liston, 2004). Moreover, as we discussed in Chapter 1, the increasingly entrepreneurial emphasis to institutional management emerging out of the Enterprise University model has, since the 1980s, brought active, commercial international marketing practices to HEIs aimed at potential applicants and partners (Gibbs, 2001; Forbes and Hamilton, 2004; Ivy and Naudé, 2004). This has led, in particular, to the rapid expansion of university international offices, populated by professional recruiters and marketers whose role is to facilitate the institutional interface with those overseas, the impact of which we will discuss in more detail in Chapter 7 (Williams, 1997; Rodwell, 1998; Humfrey, 1999).

In the light of the dramatic changes outlined above, the pace of international engagement might seem unstoppable. Indeed, the effects of an incipient international orientation to university activities have already been far-reaching. The evidence also presents a contradictory picture of internationalization, however. A range of recent press reports have noted the UK's declining share of the international student market over time, for example, reflecting perceptions about a lack of international reciprocity in British institutions compared to other global players (*Economist* 2003a, b; Blackstone, 2004; *Education Guardian*, 2005; *Times Higher Education Supplement*, 2006a, b, c, 2007a, c). Australian universities have also experienced high levels of volatility in numbers of students undertaking their studies in the country, witnessing marginal growth in recent years (IDP Education Australia, 2007). Such commentaries highlight something of a gap between the internationalist policy stance adopted in many countries and the experience of some overseas participants. As a process, therefore, HE internationalization suggests a series of tensions between expansionist government aspirations, sectoral policies marshalled towards broad commercial international engagement and the pressures experienced by academics and students inhabiting a dynamically 'internationalizing' environment. A central management concern in this context remains focused on how to respond to the volatile and uncertain dynamics of the internationalization process in order to both harness and stabilize its influence at institutional level. Yet doing so presents a range of practical and conceptual challenges. A clear first starting point in addressing the challenges of internationalization, therefore, lies with translating the conceptual themes within internationalization which we have already discussed into something that is accessible at an institutional level and open to management and policy initiatives.

A continuum of positions

One useful way of considering internationalization at institutional level, which attempts to capture both tangible and value-based aspects of the process, is as a continuum of positions from 'Symbolic' to 'Transformative' (Bartell, 2003). In this notion, Symbolic internationalization is exemplified by an institution with a basically local/national character and way of doing things, but which is populated by a proportion of overseas students and staff. At the other end of the scale, Transformative internationalization characterizes institutions where an international orientation has become 'deep', embedded into routine ways of thinking and doing, in policy and management, staff and student recruitment, curriculum and programmes (Duke, 2002; Welch, 2002):

> The reality, then, is that internationalization conveys a variety of understandings, interpretations and applications, anywhere from a minimalist, instrumental and static view, such as securing external funding for study abroad programs, through international exchange of students, conducting research internationally, to a view of internationalization as a complex, all-encompassing and policy-driven process, integral to, and permeating the life, culture, curriculum and instruction as well as research activities of the university and its members. (Bartell, 2003, p. 46)

The advantage of considering internationalization as a continuum is that it recognizes internationalization as a complex process rather than a unidimensional or static phenomenon. It also highlights the degree to which it is susceptible to management initiative rather than emerging happenstance in response to external stimuli. This is helpful where institutional managers are attempting to find coherence within a dynamic and contradictory context. The conceptual dimensions of internationalization discussed in Chapter 1 enabled a basic volumetric assessment of international activity within an institution. This is useful as an aid to understanding or in making a preliminary assessment of the extent of focus on international activity within an institution at any one time. Such static analyses do not afford a systematic approach for capturing the important qualitative aspects of the internationalization process, however, nor issues of institutional motivation or strategic thrust. Among other commentators, Bruch and Barty (1998), for example, note that internationalization requires an assessment not only of volumes of activity but also consideration of skills, attitudes, knowledge, ethos and process. The continuum therefore is a useful device for enabling discussion of less tangible aspects within the process, making explicit the longitudinal and values-based aspects of international engagement. It can also be employed as a decision-making tool, identifying and supporting strategic objective setting and organizational planning.

The key benefit of constructing operational internationalization in this way is that it emphasizes qualitative organizational inputs into the international effort and can articulate the different institutional consequences of particular combinations marshalled within specific dynamics. The institutional focus also draws on a different spectrum of literature, bringing together management practice case studies with sectoral assessments of the impact of internationalization. The context here, therefore, is essentially explanatory, delineating cause-effect implementation issues rather than operating at a definitional level.

Dimensions

Building on the preceding discussion, we will consider each of the dimensions summarized at Figure 2.1 in turn, discussing the resonances in the literature and its broad institutional implications. In employing the continuum in a practical exercise, however, it is important to recognize the clustering effect of individual dimensions. Though each dimension is discussed as discrete, the overall impact is inevitably cumulative and individual factors on the list work to reinforce and support each other. One of the most important aspects of the relationship between institution and internationalization is in its dynamic nature.

Figure 2.1: The international continuum
(adapted from Turner and Robson, 2007)

International orientation:	Symbolic	Transformative
Stimulus:	External	Internal
International impetus:	Business-led	Internationalist
Strategic management focus	Markets/ student recruitment	International partnerships/ knowledge-sharing
Financial focus:	Cost- and revenue-focused	Investment-focused
External engagement:	Competitive	Cooperative
Management style:	Designed/planned	Emergent
Institutional characterization of internationalization:	Prescriptive	Descriptive
Style of participation:	Compliance	Commitment
Sustainability	Short-term	Long-term

1. Stimulus

In considering broad issues of the style of international engagement a useful starting point is found within a retrospective assessment of its emergence. It seems clear that the impetus for the development of internationalization within an institution differs across the spectrum. Within symbolically international institutions, external globalizing drivers – notably commercial opportunities deriving from international student mobility or technologically mediated innovations in programme delivery – encourage a more outward-looking perspective within an otherwise domestic focus. In this orientation, international engagement provides a vehicle for the delivery of extrinsic rewards but is unlikely to be regarded as a strategic end in itself and may exist within a cost-minimization framework with accompanying expectations of tangible financial returns. Such an approach is consistent with globalization-led pull strategies. At the transformative end of the spectrum, however, an institution seeks to capture and organize the outward-focused energies of people within the university community – notably academics – within policy and management and invests to support that broad aim. It is clear, therefore, that internationalization can act as a descriptor of institutional culture as well as a managerial prompt for more prescriptive organizational change.

2. International impetus

Building from the first point, within either orientation potential business outcomes from internationalization are clear, in terms of revenue-generation, widening participation, international collaboration, institution building, etc. The route to the achievement of these ends will vary, however, depending on the position occupied on the continuum. A broad consensus in the literature indicates clear differences in focus between institutions which pursue internationalization within a commercial or business-related context and those whose international activities are set within a context of international development, aid, nation- or region-building or through educational development projects (Rouhani and Kishun, 2004; De Jong and Teekens, 2003; Taylor, 2004). In general, it seems clear that the external stimuli most frequently prompting explicit internationalizing activities within an institution ally to business development opportunities of some kind (Poole, 2001; Meiras, 2004). At the same time, internationalist values have long been recognized as value within liberal academic orientations (Lindahl, 2006). Some evidence also points to examples of institutional development where local academic initiatives have stimulated a broader organizational/ strategic response which is significant but not exclusively business focused in nature (Liston, 2004; Molesworth and Scullion, 2005; Postiglione, 2005). There is resonance, therefore, between the source of organizational stimulus and international positioning. A clear differentiating factor here linking to institutional values, discussed below, is the focus on organization-wide initiatives in this context. Within large and complex entities such as HEIs it is inevitable that different undertakings are likely to exist within different constituent parts of the organization, whether schools, faculties or departments. At the same time, where internationalization becomes a strategically important issue for the institution, its overall character is evident from central policy statements and institution-wide initiatives. In this way, the general strategic posture of the organization towards business or non-commercial orientations of internationalization should be reasonably clear.

3. Strategic management focus

A further broad split between international orientations which flows directly from conceptions of internationalization as either commercial or non-commercial is found in the tightness of the strategic management focus around international markets for student recruitment. Within a tightly constrained environment which is focused on the commercial benefits of internationalization, strategic attention, indicated through institutional policies, planning and target-setting, relates closely to students and programmes and is likely to have a relatively short planning horizon (see below). Within a more broadly couched orientation to international engagement, however, a wider range of strategic objectives are indicated, embracing international knowledge-development and knowledge-sharing objectives as well as those relating to the teaching mission of the institution.

4. Financial focus

Flowing directly from point three, a differentiation of financial focus is evident at the two ends of the continuum. In the Symbolic orientation, internationalization is couched as a strategic means rather than an institutional end. As we have suggested above, the evidence suggests that the business objective often takes the form of revenues generated from international projects, most commonly international student fee income derived from cross-border students studying at the host institution. Consistent with this orientation, therefore, the symbolic approach to internationalization shows a clear focus on those revenues and is also concerned with cost minimization in order to maximize financial or other business returns. In this way, international students are assimilated into provision based on existing institutional models, supports provided for them are limited, international employees may be recruited as part of a cost-minimization policy and resource deployment for international ventures is limited to activities which are able to show a direct financial return, such as student recruitment and marketing. At the Transformative end of the continuum, however, a focus is maintained in which long-term partnerships, scholar exchanges and research collaborations are supported as investments which may not show a direct financial return and international activities are integrated into the broad educational and intellectual mission of the institution rather than simply within its financial or revenue-earning systems.

5. External engagement

A further dimension in conceiving of internationalization is the degree to which universities have approached it from a competitive or cooperative perspective (Van der Wende, 2001; Chan, 2004; Luijten-Lub *et al.*, 2005). Within this analysis the market-driven competitive positioning adopted by universities in many Anglophone countries differentiates from the international orientation within non-Anglo, European institutions, which have focused on international knowledge-sharing, cooperation and engagement. From this perspective, the Anglo approach emphasizes revenue-focused activities such as overseas student recruitment, the development of transnational projects and commercial partnerships (De Vita and Case, 2003; Molesworth and Scullion, 2005). In general, the cooperative orientation relates to internationalist principles reflecting the value-based aspects of the Transformative end of the continuum and challenging the ability of the competitive approach in achieving effective long-term international engagement:

> [The] discourse of marketization . . . promotes effects that militate against a type of internationalisation that would make university culture more multicultural, more open to the other and more conducive to the development of a critical stance vis-à-vis our own cultural conditioning and national prejudices. (De Vita and Case, 2003, p. 384)

6. Management style

Given the basic divergence in strategic thrust within Symbolic and Transformative internationalization – top-down, management and business-led vs. bottom-up, academic and knowledge-sharing-led – it seems clear that the management style that is evident within each orientation also differs. Within the Symbolic orientation, management and policy approaches tend to design for internationalization within the context of conventional rational planning. On the other hand, Transformative internationalization shows evidence of emergent approaches to management, attempting to coordinate and orchestrate diverse local initiatives, bringing institutional coherence. It also seems clear that in this orientation, active planning and management of internationalization is retrospective to a larger degree, responding to pre-existing organizational events whereas Symbolic internationalization anticipates institution-wide activity and prompts this from the centre. Clearly, the particular character of the relationship between individual work units and the central institutional administration varies within this context. Nonetheless, the practice-based literature suggests a clear divide in the respective softness and flexibility of management approaches at either end of the spectrum.

7. Institutional characterization of internationalization

In harmony with point 6, differences emerge at the ends of the continuum in the degree of flexibility ascribed to internationalization. As such, internationalization can be either prescriptive or descriptive. Symbolic internationalization characterizes prescriptive managerial action which is policy- and 'business'-led, while Transformative internationalization is a descriptive phenomenon in which the personal and ideological commitment of the university community stimulates the institution's international policies and practices. On the one hand, symbolically international institutions, having made a planned international commitment within a wider strategic focus and anticipating the desired outcomes, tightly manage progress to the achievement of that objective. This directs institutional energies in clearly definable areas and is consistent with the development of planned intention. Little divergence is permitted and work units and individuals may be held accountable for achievements against targets, e.g. for international student recruitment. Transformative institutions, on the other hand, show a more flexible approach to their characterization of international engagement, consistent with broadly focused international objectives. The formal articulation of international objectives may be as clear but, given that the ends sought from international engagement are more generally articulated, achievements are assessed more qualitatively and are more open-ended.

8. Style of participation

For academic managers, a central consideration within the broader continuum of positions is how far an institution seeks *Compliance with* – indicating behavioural conformity with stated institutional policy but no inevitable requirement for a particular shift in personal or social values or practices – or *Commitment to* – where social and personal values have shifted to an ethnorelative perspective aligning behaviours as well – its international orientation. What's fairly clear from the literature is that Transformative internationalization is *personal* not *institutional*, what's been called 'Existential Internationalization': as much about academics' personal world-views as about anything that is achievable managerially (Sanderson, 2004). In this context, a clear alignment between individuals' personal values and the institutional orientation seems a prerequisite in sustaining international effort. Equally, the literature indicates that activity within symbolically international institutions is often ritualistic, positioning internationalization as a vehicle for the achievement of other, tangible strategic objectives (revenue-generation, recruitment volumes, programme development, etc.). In reality, internationalization merely captures a set of values and beliefs – ethical and ideological – held by its communities which privilege either cultural diversity or cultural exclusivity. At the same time, a focus on practical long-term international sustainability, whether in terms of overseas student recruitment or teaching and research collaborations, requires the alignment of institutional policies with both resources and people's commitment.

9. Sustainability

Building on the above discussion, inevitable resonances emerge between long-term sustainability in terms of international engagement and those dimensions indicated towards the Transformative end of the continuum. Ultimately Transformative internationalization emerges in an institution iteratively generated by the internationalist energies and enthusiasms of individual people at a local level and the management and policy stimulus provided organizationally. Symbolic internationalization both configures international engagement in a narrow way, usually focused on the limits of particular marketplaces, and subordinates internationalist individual and organizational energies to more specific business ends.

One of the most intractable challenges for university managers in addressing internationalization, therefore, lies in building impetus for fundamental long-term behavioural and values-based change within an institution while maintaining a focus on current business deliverables. As we will discuss in Chapter 3, this conjunction of the practice and values-based aspects of Transformative internationalization constitutes something of a departure from traditional management practices. Human resource development initiatives, for example, have rarely focused on the personal – which might be regarded as intrusive – but tend to emphasize behavioural compliance and skills development. Equally, it seems clear that much of what constitutes accepted cultural practice in a given local context remains largely implicit and, therefore, relatively unsusceptible to explicit management initiative. At the same time, if we accept that internationalization in its most fundamental sense is reshaping both the intellectual and educational context of HE around the world, then some shift towards Transformative internationalization seems both inevitable and necessary for broadly based HEIs. The management task, therefore, lies in facilitating change in ways that can support the institution's wider organizational aims.

Given the linkage between commercial orientation and business ends it seems clear that a key consideration in the area of sustainability is the degree to which the returns from international effort are regarded as extrinsic. If internationalization is regarded as an investment vehicle in order to secure either institutional expansion or revenue generation, the international initiatives must compete with alternative business objectives. The strategic horizon of such an approach is necessarily foreshortened therefore, to the point at which more lucrative alternative developments are undertaken. On the other hand, if internationalization is regarded as an integral part of the institution's identity, whether bringing a commercial return or not, its longevity as an influence within the institution is considerably extended. Ultimately, at the Symbolic end of the continuum, internationalization is regarded as something an institution *does* while for a Transformative institution it is something it *is*.

Clustering

Organizations often evaluate their level of internationalization through an assessment of one of the more obvious dimensions, notably the presence of international students and the fee revenues they bring. Certainly building student and academic mobility is an important indicator, as we have discussed. A reliance on one or two aspects within the continuum, however, may not attest to anything other than temporary and short-lived international engagement and certainly does not speak of more fundamental internationalization. For example, the presence of mass numbers of international students, mainly from the 'South' in 'Northern' HEIs tends to be an indicator of a particular stage of economic and social development in a number of sending countries and a corresponding lack of domestic HE provision. Where a perceived premium is attached to HE attainments and local provision is unable to fulfil that need, students with access to the financial means will travel to achieve the premium. The evidence seems clear that local provision can fairly quickly develop to respond to the gap, however, at first from a range of transnational projects and partnerships and ultimately through the development of direct locally owned provision. Examples of this are clear in the People's Republic of China (PRC), with a flourishing of both public and private-sector programmes in the past ten years. Thus, if Northern HEIs measure their internationalization mainly by international student flows and the provision of services to support them, it is unlikely to indicate either deep or sustainable levels of internationalization. Instead, the underlying emphasis in the literature indicates clearer international resonances from the ways in which HEIs respond to internationalizing knowledge production in its broadest sense. This is found in levels of international research and other educational partnerships and activities. Again it is not so much a sense of behavioural levels of activity but in the orientation towards these partnerships – an emphasis on knowledge-sharing and development rather than transfer, of reciprocity rather than 'conceptual colonialism' (Biggs, 2003; Sanderson, 2004). If any sense of the long-lasting or fundamental implications of internationalization is to be found as opposed to its existing as a fleeting migratory phenomenon, then it is here in the area of social learning, development and international inclusivity. Fundamentally, therefore, it is for this reason that an emphasis on the affective and values-based aspects of internationalization is important. It is certainly clear that HEIs which adopt an activity-based assessment of their international position could be classed as international at any one time. If one is making an assessment of more profound levels of internationalization, however, systems, attitudes and motivations provide the evidence rather than any individual group of activities.

Positioning, rhetoric and reality

The key underlying consideration when assessing international positioning on the continuum is that it operates descriptively. Indeed, from Bartell's (2003) perspective, all positions on the continuum are valid. The issue confronting university managers and communities is consciously to reflect on their context and determine how they want to position themselves and move within it. Some institutions across the world have opted for a tight focus on a very local context and to work within a specific environment rather than opening up to wider 'international' opportunities, for example such as private-sector commercial colleges in the USA (Morey, 2004). This has enabled them to target specific local student and staff constituencies and engage in academic partnerships that are consonant with their focused institutional mission. Others have incorporated a specifically commercial, revenue-generating international subsidiary to their wider local activities (De Jong and Teekens, 2003). On the other hand, most broadly based Anglophone universities have rhetorically postured towards more Transformative internationalization. At the same time, the evidence suggests that actual institutional engagement varies across the continuum, however, resulting from inherent tensions between internationalist values and competitive approaches. Within this context one of the key institutional issues to address is the alignment of rhetoric with the reality of engagement. Frequent gaps between how institutions talk about international engagement and what their policies and practices actually do, therefore appear. Schapper and Mayson (2004, p. 191), for example, have characterized international strategy implementation in some Australian universities as 'crude', as the market-driven orientation of institutional policy confronts the values manifest within the academic community. Turner and Robson (2007) have discussed the cynicism with which an internationalist academic community in the UK responded to institutional student recruitment targets which they believed privileged revenue-generation over educational considerations. De Jong and Teekens (2003) describe problematic outcomes as long-term gradualist approaches adopted by an institution in the Netherlands were superseded by bolt-on commercial international initiatives in the 1990s. What seems clear from these examples is the potential for difficulties where internationalist rhetoric clashes with a more commercially driven implementation or where commercial motivations do not fully take into account either ethical or educational considerations.

Willing engagement

The difficulty here seems to lie not only in the dynamics of internationalization as a process but, particularly in market-focused environments, in the problem of departing from 'the pack' in responding to the internationalization challenge. In the UK, for example, government policy in the form of the Prime Minister's Initiatives, promoting international engagement in 1999 and 2006 (DfES, 2006; British Council, 2007), have been key national drivers in developing an international thrust of engagement in the sector. In this environment, institutions working at the Symbolic end of the continuum may feel that they are being driven towards internationalization rather than embarking upon wider international engagement willingly – especially in delivering policy expectations about, e.g., international student participation in degree-level studies. In such contexts, the danger is of increasing variation between public statements and policies and the actuality of engagement. In these circumstances an increasingly cynical orientation to internationalization may develop which both limits its potential and can risk damaging staff morale and institutional reputation. At the very least, a minimalist orientation to internationalization seems evident. Inevitably such an orientation tends to regard internationalization as a temporary externally driven phenomenon rather than as a catalyst for permanent change in the nature of HE.

Internationalization as a process

Notwithstanding the implications of the preceding discussion, in the short term, the long-term 'destination' on the continuum is likely to be subordinated to the process accompanying its development. Providing opportunities for university people to participate in discussion and become involved in determining the scope, penetration and content of an 'internationalization' agenda seems a necessary prerequisite for 'success', however it is measured and inevitable in any shift towards the Transformative end of the continuum. This is particularly important given the personal and psychological elements inherent in Transformative internationalization, as people move from an ethnocentric to an ethnorelative orientation in their academic lives in order to embrace it (Bennett, 1993):

> The need to explain why internationalization . . . is an important issue, and an especially important one for an organization such as a

university, is a primary requirement that needs to be in place prior to the systematic development of strategies. Academics generally require compelling reason and argument before accepting any institutional strategy. (Webb, 2005, p. 109)

Within the management and policy arena, concerns about the value of international reciprocity and inclusivity are sometimes marginalized against business concerns of revenue-generation, marketing and sustainable overseas student recruitment (Mackinnon, 1998; Meek, 2000; De Vita and Case, 2003). Conversely, teaching and learning concerns focus on the practical challenges inherent in classroom diversity and the development of inclusive educational strategies to manage the consequences of both international and domestic massification (Kember, 2000; Le Roux, 2002; Biggs, 2003). Commentators have noted that these two themes are often at odds with each other, resulting in tensions between management objectives and effective educational practices. Welch (2002), for example, notes that organizational/managerial discourse stresses educational reciprocity as the motivation in many Anglophone HE contexts, while the reality as organizationally planned and experienced by people within university communities relates more narrowly to revenue-generation, markets and student recruitment. This aspect of the discourse resonates with other HE debates, problematizing the introduction of quasi-commercial practices and characterizing HE as in a globalization-generated crisis of identity (Deem, 2001; Watson, 2002). A clear focus on internationalization as a process of change, therefore, helps to stabilize some of these tensions, to reinforce the need for dialogue and engagement and to minimize the tendency to focus on an analysis based on an assessment of prevailing conditions at any one time.

An international institution:
how would you know one when you see one?

The outcome of the discussions in Chapters 1 and 2 lead us to a position where it is both possible to understand internationalization conceptually and to undertake an assessment of both qualitative motivations, the issue of strategic thrust and management within institutions. As the basic institutional frameworks of policy and practice that respond to internationalization become clear, the outline of different forms of international organization emerges. This is an important first step in enabling us to identify what an international

HEI might be. In arriving at a more complete understanding of an international institution, however, it is also essential to begin to penetrate the more problematic implications of Transformative internationalization and sustainability. In this context, Sanderson's (2004) notion of 'existential internationalization' is foregrounded. Within an overall framework of international effort it seems clear that the personal engagement and positive motivations of individual people within an institution are not only essential in securing a shift to the ethnorelative position inherent in deep internationalization orientations but are also prerequisites for long-term international engagement at an institutional level. To that extent, therefore, an international institution is recognizable from within its own psyche – deep internationalization acts normatively on the values and practices of institutional communities, shifting individual and institutional orientations towards existential internationalization. What seems clear from the evidence is that whether for business or knowledge-sharing reasons, large institutions in many contexts are aiming at such long-term engagement and are seeking to normalize the organizational discourse of internationalization as well as develop systems and practices to support it. Thus an international institution emerges as one which manages not only its practices and policies but also is explicit about its values and beliefs (Stone, 2006). As we have implied throughout these first two chapters, however, profound implications for academic values and practices arise from such changes. Chapter 3, therefore, goes on to discuss the educational and pedagogical aspects of internationalization and its broad implications for diversity.

Chapter 3

Internationalization: the challenges

The challenges of internationalization: local practices in an international context

The previous chapters have concentrated their discussions on broad definitions of internationalization as a phenomenon and have sought to clarify its key conceptual and organizational dimensions. These discussions, however, do not necessarily acknowledge many of the intellectual challenges that are inherent in the evolution of internationalization. This chapter explores more closely the nature of the practical, pedagogical and epistemological challenges that are embedded within increasing internationalization, particularly within the management of academic activities. It begins by discussing the challenges of moving from a locally determined and implicit set of ethnocentric pedagogic values towards a more explicitly ethnorelative position and then discusses examples of the range of different constructs of higher learning and education around the world. The chapter goes on to consider the implications of this variety to internationalization efforts within institutions and assesses the implications of existential internationalization for university communities, management and institutional structures and systems.

Education is culturally situated: local vs. international

As we have indicated in Chapter 1, most of the history of HE points to the national rather than the international and has been concerned with nation-building, national economic development and civic society (Scott, 1998; Teichler, 1996, 1998; deWit, 2002; Bleiklie and Powell, 2005). Universities, therefore, experience a basic struggle in attempting to internationalize. On the one hand, the academic role of HE in knowledge-sharing and development is inherently regional or international. On the other, the political, financial and institutional context of that knowledge development and a fundamentally local construction of educational purpose remains nationally defined. Universities have always worked to meet the two ends whether in finding the balance between state intervention and academic freedom and autonomy or in responding to the conflicting requirements to provide locally relevant education as well as globally competent graduates. At the same time, in practice, local issues have frequently overwhelmed broader international concerns, particularly where national funding structures continue to hold significant sway. For example, HE internationalization is intimately linked with massification. Debate about massification has largely focused on local issues – primarily widening participation for local minority groups – however, rather than grappling with the implications of international diversity and participation, outward internationalization and an increasingly mixed economy of local and national sources of funding (Scott, 1998; Peters, 2004).

Scope of the impact

In spite of the dominance of the local in many areas of the educational life of HEIs, acknowledging that international knowledge flows have been a permanent feature of the HE landscape demonstrates that internationalization in its broadest sense is not really a new phenomenon. What is new, however, is the scale of contemporary international engagement and the extent to which international systems are influencing HEIs' local institutional, organizational and financial systems as well as their academic and educational practices. The implications of the step-change seem clear. In the past HEIs have embodied the social and intellectual spirit of a particular nation state and to a large extent the processes and products of HE have been defined within national contexts and shaped according to local need and utility. Now, however, fundamental questions of a practical as well as intellectual nature confront HEIs about the relevance and contribution of their activities in both local and international fora (AUT/DEA, 1999; McKenzie *et al.*, 2003; Gabb, 2006). Problematically, HEIs need to define themselves and their values within an internationally relevant context while at the same time continuing to meet local educational needs. Clear conflicts can result. In developing countries, for example, universities which are re-shaping courses and curricula along international lines might at one and the same time contribute to improving the national skills base and global competitiveness as well as to skills depletion and brain drain as skilled graduates emigrate elsewhere (Yan, 1998; Yang, 2002; Zweig *et al.*, 2004). Equally, in many post-industrial nations the expansion of commercial international programmes and projects can work against the underlying internationalist values of knowledge-sharing and multilateral educational development (Welch, 2002; Woolf, 2002). Ultimately the struggle worked out between the idiosyncrasies of local context and international demand introduces a significant tension not only into the dynamics of the discourse of internationalization but also stresses potential contradictions in practices and the determination of operational priorities.

Implicitly cultural practices and pedagogies

The tensions that exist between sometimes competing requirements of local and international intrude deeply into considerations of academic practices. The term internationalization implies that national distinctiveness and local context are still a central influence on practice. The issue focuses on managing the balance between national distinctiveness and international inclusivity. At the same time, relatively little discussion in the literature has explored underlying assumptions behind everyday teaching practices or problematized pedagogy from a cultural perspective. Indeed, to a large extent the cultural foundations of local pedagogies remain implicit:

> Administrators, academics and students are so much socialized to take the national conditions of HE for granted that they are hardly aware of the extent to which they are national rather than global 'players'. (Teichler, 1998, p. 88)

> Western views on individual rights and individual autonomy lead to distinctive assumptions about how learning takes place. (Woodrow, 2001, p. 23)

Even the growing numbers of commentators developing critiques of dominant pedagogical approaches have tended to concentrate more on practice issues rather than reflecting on the cultural values and beliefs underpinning contemporary epistemologies or the contingent sociology of national educational systems (Thorstensson, 2001; Hanassab and Tidwell, 2002; Carroll and Ryan, 2005). To some extent, this may result from a generally untheorized pedagogical context for many HE teaching practices, for example, which has facilitated the continued dominance of local, ethnocentric 'folk pedagogies' (Simon, 1999; Bruner, 1999; Gabb, 2006). Nonetheless, it is widely recognized that knowledge traditions and pedagogical values emerged from cultural and historical contexts that shaped them in particular ways and reflect the societies in which they found their evolution (Brown, 1998; Batelaan and Gundare, 2000; Murphy and Ivinson, 2003). In addition, the histories from which modern epistemological belief systems developed were defined by eclectic and isolationist local information contexts (Smith, 1998). European/Christian and Asian/Buddhist/ Confucianist epistemologies followed very different evolutionary paths, for example. Such differences brought with them all sorts of sociological and pedagogical impacts, including the idiosyncratic character and social role of scientific enquiry and the processes and styles employed to legitimate the articulation of intellectual thought, particularly in the nature of argument and writing (Woo, 1993). To some degree the increased international knowledge-transfer that has taken place in the past 50 years has encouraged convergence in style and approach across the world, sometimes at the cost of cultural identity, as we discussed in Chapter 1. Nonetheless, the impact of differing locally defined knowledge traditions still influences many aspects of intellectual life, particularly in the implicit assumptions governing academic practices within HE. Institutions, therefore, need to reassess apparently universalist 'Western' pedagogical assumptions in the light of increasing international engagement in order to develop more inclusive, reciprocal approaches towards both knowledge-sharing and teaching and learning practices within culturally diverse academies (Hills and Thom, 2005; Tatar, 2005; Hanassab, 2006).

HE Pedagogy

In essence, the discourse of Anglo-European HE pedagogy remains implicitly cultural and unchanging rather than plural and is possessed of strong normative assumptions (Bruner, 1996, 1999; Hufton *et al.*, 2002). Accounts recognize pluralism in content to a greater extent than within intellectual structures and processes, especially in their treatment of styles and approaches to learning taken in other countries (Hill *et al.*, 2000; Braine, 2002). This is particularly the case in relatively normative applied disciplines such as business and management studies, for example, where classroom routines can tend to reinforce the Anglo-European cultural and ideological foundations of the discipline (Mackinnon, 1998; Case and Selvester, 2000, 2002; Ottewill and Macfarlane, 2003). The practical impacts are numerous. As we will explore in the following chapters, evidence exists of widely held prejudices among university teachers in many Anglophone countries about certain educational behaviours and practices regarded as 'non-Western' or 'surface' in spite of some evidence pointing to the long-term contribution that such techniques can make to the development of deeper learning (Woo, 1993; Leung, 2001; Asmar, 2005; Marton *et al.*, 2005). Across a broad range, research suggests the persistence of educational and organizational practices which reinforce the privileging of colloquial local self-stereotypes alongside negative stereotypes of cultural outsiders who participate in local systems (Pritchard and Skinner, 2002; Burke, 2006). A key issue here is the degree to which the normative constructions of education tend to be highly implicit, silently obstructing accessibility to non-local participants and, importantly, undervaluing the benefits of cultural reciprocity within both educational and intellectual contexts. In particular such an implicit privileging of local values characterizes internationalization in particular ways – as a unidirectional flow of influence from host countries outwards – encouraging the persistence of increasingly out-of-date, unreflected-upon local constructions of the function of HE which ignore the inward implications of diversity and international development (Robertson, Line, Jones and Thomas, 2000). Such approaches have been variously called 'deficit', 'accommodation' approaches, 'conceptual colonialism' or 'colonialism of the mind' (Biggs, 2003; Egege and Kutieleh, 2003; Meiras, 2004), broadly stylizing hegemonic flows of cultural influence from North and West to South and East, reflecting descriptions about incipient 'Westernization' in the context of HE internationalization. Essentially the persistence of such intellectual assumptions ignore the active tension that exists between the local, isolationist histories governing HE's evolution and the multinational, multicultural dynamics of the contemporary environment (Singh, 2002). This underplays the importance of so-called Internationalization at Home and resonates closely with the parallel challenges of widening local participation and multi-cultural diversity (Asmar, 2005; Wachter, 2003). As indicated by De Vita and Case (2003), much of the energy given to internationalization in UK HE, for example, has focused on the inclusion of 'international' themes in the content of the curriculum at the expense of broader pedagogic treatments. This approach, they assert, treats internationalization as an exclusively cognitive matter. The wider implications of an international perspective, however, are values-based as much as cognitive and involve personal and social learning as well as intellectual engagement:

> Managing participation within an institutional setting is a matter of resolving conflicts between the various social norms experienced by

learners in the communities they engage in. The social norms and values encountered in these communities, such as family, peer group and friendship groups, are taken up by students and influence their negotiation and management of their participation and, hence, their learning in classroom settings. (Murphy and Ivinson, 2003, p. 6)

In essence, intercultural exchange is transacted, and is not simply a discourse. An emphasis on internationalizing curriculum content without the development of social intercultural practices and exchange may encourage participants – both students and teachers – to objectify and compartmentalize internationalization, potentially undermining its more fundamental reflective and reflexive educational contribution (Crabtree and Sapp, 2004).

East and West: social constructions of educational cultures

Within this broad discussion, one of the key dichotomies articulated in the Anglophone literature is between 'Asian' and 'Anglo' education systems and their attitudes to the learning process. In the Anglophone literature, Asian students, for example, are frequently stereotyped as passive, unreflective learners who tend towards an instrumental approach to learning, while their Anglo counterparts are described as active, critical and self-managing independent learners (Dooley, 2004; Radbourne, 2006). Such stereotypes have, of course, been increasingly criticized (Volet and Chalmers, 1997; Kember, 2000; Turner, 2006a, b). The tendency still persists, however, to attempt to support Asian cross-border learners over the 'learning transition' and effectively initiate them into the dominant Anglo culture of the academy. Much of this discussion ignores a deeper reality. Firstly, that both Asian and Anglo learners require initiation into the learned cultures of academies. Secondly, it ignores the fact that historically intellectual cultures across Asia have been highly influential on the development of Anglo-European modes of thought and educational practices. The cultural superiority of one approach over another is fallacious, therefore. Rather, national educational cultures exist in a context of dynamic, reciprocal relationships (Bruner, 1996; Brown, 1998; Halstead, 2004).

One of the hinges of this differentiation between Asian and Anglo learners lies in how prime academic relationships – between lecturers and students, for example – are constructed. Asian students are widely regarded as being highly dependent on the lecturer, while Anglo students are regarded as less so and able to function independently. Within the individualist societies of the West the historical apotheosis of the academic or intellectual is the independent (usually secular) and autonomous autodidact, working essentially alone and maintaining a 'scientifically sceptical' stance on society in order to effect social change through the act of critique (Brown, 1998). Such characterizations of intellectual life have been far less evident within 'Asian' societies across the world, influenced as they are by the collectivist values of Confucianism, Buddhism and Islam, for example (Parmenter, 1999; Halstead, 2004; Hui, 2005). It is important to note two things, however. Firstly, that critique is not entirely absent in 'Eastern' societies – it can and does take place – but that the styles and mechanisms for its engagement and articulation are different (Kim, 2003). Secondly, that the cognitive and technical aspects of critical scientific enquiry are very much in evidence even within relatively authoritarian societies across the world (Brown, 1998). The issue of dependence on the role of the mentor or educator has significant importance as stylistic differentiator between East and West (Hui, 2005). Fundamentally, the key issues focus on the stage at which autonomy and critical engagement is regarded as appropriate and how far they are stylistic and substantive behaviours. In Western countries intellectual autonomy is generally regarded as arriving much earlier in life than in the East (Turner, 2006b). This derives from the intimate holistic correlation between intellectual and spiritual development that characterizes many Eastern educational philosophies and the degree to which intellectual traditions ascribe learning as truly 'lifelong' rather than confined within the formal education process. In many Asian countries where learning is regarded as lifelong, the intellectual community has developed a generally gerontocratic character, while in Anglo societies youth and formal education are regarded as more significant. Equally in Western societies, social criticism is intimately bound up within archetypes of the intellectual community to a far greater extent than may be the case elsewhere.

Overall, it is easy to see the roots of differences in conceptions of important roles and behaviours in the HE environment. The basic character of local academic society in which education is situated intimately shapes the dynamics of the teaching and learning process taking place in the classroom (Kempner and Makino, 1993; Singh, 2002). In the Anglo context therefore – and especially for social scientists – great emphasis is placed upon individualism, argumentation, linking propositional and procedural knowledges together, intellectual and personal transformation and the application of the products of intellectual engagement onto society while remaining intellectually independent from it. In some respects, this presents a radicalizing or iconoclastic notion of intellectual life. Within

Asian constructs, more of an emphasis is placed upon the development of the intellectual community, reflection and contemplation of intellectual ideas, building upon and developing synthesis within existing intellectual thought as part of society. This presents more of a harmonizing perspective to intellectual life. If the broader character of the intellectual community reflects these basic characteristics and operates within such different social constructs, it is hardly surprising that the rules of engagement that operate within HEIs also differ radically. Crossing boundaries between academies, therefore, brings as many attributes of culture shock as crossing geographical boundaries yet the nature of the differences can often remain obscure because they are so highly implicit (Seo and Koro-Ljungberg, 2005).

Setting aside such broad sociological differences in the characteristics and value of intellectual life, the reality remains that all participants in HE, whether international or not require orientation into cultures within local academies, as indicated above. Essentially, cultural insiders and outsiders are not very different from each other in this respect – after all, 'academic language . . . is no one's mother tongue' (Bourdieu and Passeron, 1996, p. 8). At the same time, the personal and emotional responses individuals make to the environments they encounter inevitably differ according to their pre-existing cognitive schema – predisposed by previous educational experiences – and are governed by very different cultural ideas about interpersonal behaviour and etiquette. The key tensions between local models of learning, therefore, are not exclusively located in the behaviour of participants who are not local, but are also found in the attitudes and responses of cultural insiders to those who do not conform to their implicit expectations. Evidence from the Anglo-European literature suggests that negative perceptions about divergence from implicit local norms of behaviour tend to compound stereotypes of certain groups of 'Asian' students who approach the learning task in different (quiet, passive-receptive, reflective) ways to those behaviours privileged locally (active, participative) (Volet and Chalmers, 1997; Kember, 2000) . As a result such students are often characterized as a 'problem' and in response to their perceived needs teachers adopt so-called deficit or accommodation approaches, discussed above, to enable them to participate effectively within local norms of behaviour (Biggs, 2003). Importantly, these can lead to the articulation in practice of unreflected-upon colloquial models of teaching, learning and development in fundamental areas such as critical thinking. In this context important substantive cognitive and skills capabilities are lumped together with culturally stylistic behaviours in a confused and contradictory notion of what characterizes meaningful deeper or higher learning (Turner, 2006b). This can result in confusion about academic expectations and conflates learning development and cultural academic conventions. In doing so, it can lengthen the learning transition for students, limit international knowledge-sharing and unthinkingly bring ideological attributes within HE to the fore, driving 'conceptual colonialism'. In a practical sense a reliance upon such implicit local notions of learning can lead academic practitioners rhetorically to fall back upon poorly articulated conceptions of, for example, 'critical thinking' within their espoused pedagogy while not actively translating them into their pedagogies-in-use. Thus Biggs (2003), among others, argues that in spite of value statements within the Anglophone academic practice literature suggesting that critical thinking is a core component of the HE curriculum, the majority of assessment in practice focuses on the declarative not the critical. Brown (1998) too notes the tendency to ignore the socio-cultural roots of learning indicators such as 'critical' thinking and to confuse it with problem solving and other more truly universal cognitive skills, with the consequence that lecturers can encourage students to develop stylistic skills which are useful in one social context but redundant in many others.

Some of the tendency to define divisions between Anglo and Asian characterizations of education and learning also derive from static rather than dynamic notions of learners which characterize – and stereotype – international learners on the basis of their approach when they first arrive in the host institution rather than after they have undergone the learning transitions of the first few months (Egege and Kutieleh, 2003; Walker, 2004). This tendency also resonates with a general perspective in confronting international diversity to focus on *differences* rather than *similarities* between learners. Layered into general 'deficit' approaches, this tendency not only focuses attention and debate about cultural insiders vs. cultural 'others', it also puts the onus for change on new entrants to make adaptations. Importantly, it reduces the potential to recognize positive contributions from different orientations to learning, limits the development of composite, complex models of deeper learning which ignore the importance of cognitive and skills development for local students who will live and work in an internationally integrated environment. Ultimately these tendencies contribute to the development of implicit therapeutic or remedial perspectives in respect of the management of classroom diversity, which characterize much of the literature about those who are perceived as 'different' from the normative local stereotype. The academic practice literature is littered with examples of how to 'accommodate' non-conforming participants, make them 'better' and 'fit' into the dominant way of doing things so that they can work within the perceived norms of the local community, and discussions about the risks of doing so (Gatfield *et al.*, 1999; Hanassab and Tidwell, 2002; Butcher and McGrath, 2004; Dooley, 2004; Camiciotolli, 2005; Radbourne, 2006). The association of such notions with the 'blame the student' culture are well rehearsed but not only do they place an emphatic responsibility on 'cultural others' to 'get better', they also facilitate a continued privileging of local pedagogies and maintain the academic – literally the 'doctor' – as the expert mediator in initiating students into the narrow particulars of local academic cultures.

This debate is set up as a normalizing dichotomy between cultural insiders and outsiders. If one accepts a constructionist view of learning, however, then context, social community and educational design, including pedagogy, all carry a greater weight of responsibility to 'scaffold' and mediate the learners' development than the students themselves. What is clear is that the two incipient forces of massification and internationalization of HE are driving increasing cohort diversity and forcing academic practitioners to rethink their beliefs about the nature of learning (Deardorff, 2006; Stone, 2006). University teachers are beginning to recognize the limitation of local folk pedagogies and distinguish between cultural stylistic and substantive matters within their notions of teaching and learning. However:

> Mass HE systems have to go deeper and wider . . . in the sense that they must take great account of non-western intellectual traditions, or perhaps better, the growing pluralism within the western tradition . . . Just as they must cope with social pluralism, so they must confront intellectual pluralism. (Scott, 1998, pp. 120–1)

Institutional practices

Implicit cultural norms do not only saturate academic practices within HE, they also have a significant impact on institutional systems and infrastructure. For example, factors within admissions processes are often culturally weighted. Acceptance on a programme of study implies a psychological and actual or legal contract between institution and applicant. In spite of the very broad nature of general entry standards to HEIs, therefore, applicants are likely to take acceptance on a programme as an institutional acknowledgement that they have a reasonable chance of successfully completing their course of study. At the same time, high levels of cultural difference in local interpretations of the meaning of acceptance on a programme of study and the anticipated outcome also exist. Within the UK context, for example, the relationship between university and student has traditionally rested on the student achieving certain measured competence in their chosen programme of study, one in which success is contingent upon both the commitment and ultimate capability of the student (Ottewill and MacFarlane, 2003). In this context, students can and do fail courses of study. The local convention implies that students themselves individually accept the major responsibility for their academic success (Biggs, 2003). This is consistent with the prevailing construct of university students as adult, independent learners and links to a sociological construction of the nature of intelligence that suggests that it is in part innate, unequally distributed and individually developed (Claxton, 1996a, b; Barnett, 1997). Such a notion of educational achievement is by no means universal, however. Indeed in many Asian societies the philosophical and educational traditions discussed above have influenced a construct of intelligence derived more from hard work and application than innate ability, one which is more community-centred and extrinsic than the individualist, intrinsic perspective taken in 'the West' (Woo, 1993; Szalay *et al.*, 1994; Kim, 2003). In such contexts, responsibility for student success is very widely distributed, with teachers and institutions ultimately accountable rather than individuals. These influences are compounded in countries such as China – a key sending country for contemporary cross-border HE programmes – with its egalitarian socialist dynamic during the twentieth century, highly influenced by Marxian ideals about the openness of knowledge and humankind's universal developmental capacity (Turner and Acker, 2002). Islamic notions of education also differ sharply from the Anglo-European, fostering community responsibility for learning within a specific religious moral and ethical framework (Halstead, 2004).

Such cultural differences have a clear influence on the nature of the implied contract that exists between student and institution. In practice, in many Asian countries failure to obtain a degree is highly unusual, for example. Assessment practices and systems are designed to give maximum support and provide numerous opportunities for students to retake 'failed' assignments. Lecturers' professional success is often intimately connected with the achievements of their students (Turner and Acker, 2002). Direct responsibility for student success is commonly considered to lie with the teacher rather than the student, therefore:

In Chinese [there is] a saying. 'There is no bad student, just a bad teacher.' . . . Because every student, every people, they can learn. Why they didn't learn well, maybe is the method of the teacher . . . the teacher has some problems. They cannot teach the student well. (Turner, 2006a, p. 40)

In such an environment, acceptance into a programme of study not only implies a willing commitment between institution and student that all will do their best, but forms a much stronger guarantee of success than is usually the case in countries like the UK.

Inconsistencies emerge not only from general admissions processes but also attach to particular criteria adopted. The use of English language test scores as a measure for admissions is highly problematic, for example, has been shown to be inherently variable and a poor predictor of academic success (Seelen, 2002). Equally, researchers have noted that teachers in Anglophone universities have tended to proxy language competence for indicators of broader intellectual ability, influencing their perspectives on particular students (Le Roux, 2001; Sanderson, 2004). Indeed, the false expectations raised by an admissions emphasis on language competence has been shown to contribute to wider negative stereotypes of many Asian students (Samuelowicz and Bain, 2001; Devos, 2003; Walker, 2004). This has occurred in the face of evidence indicating that, in terms of students' overall motivation, learning preferences and development, local students and their cross-border counterparts engage with education in a similar manner (Ramburuth and McCormick, 2001; Braine, 2002). Indeed, research into the Chinese Learner Paradox shows that over the long term Asian students regularly out-perform their Anglophone counterparts, irrespective of the language medium of instruction (Marton *et al.*, 2005).

Implications

Taking all these factors into account, it is clear that, in spite of acknowledged learner diversity in HE, a range of factors – including the homogenizing tendency of institutional systems such as admissions, disciplinary norms and the privileging of cultural academic models and conventions – coalesce together to militate against its explicit recognition in routine practices. Often new arrivals tend to be left alone to figure out how to function in the local context (Braine, 2002). If they do so and are able to work confidently within prevailing cultural norms, then they may go on to achieve adequately – fortunately many do. Inevitably some are likely to become cultural casualties within the educational process, however, and are unsuccessful in their academic efforts. Many more may underachieve, resulting in less obvious but damaging impacts on their self-confidence as well as their marks. More insidiously, if left implicit, such educational practices reinforce negative stereotypes about categories of cross-border students compared to those who are local. It may often seem simpler to approach the HE task as if the community was unified and homogeneous. Certainly many admissions systems linked to the prevailing unitarism evident within Anglophone HE environments tend to encourage the sense of a direct equivalence between one educational system and another, one individual and another. The reality, however, is that such approaches both ignore the complexity of skills involved in intercultural working and managing diversity and accept the dominance of particular cultural models of educational practice around the world. Moreover, if one accepts social constructionist analyses of learning – stressing its situated and collective development – the issues emerge as more profound than simple cultural variations in educational practices and accept that the basic fabric and substance of learning is culturally situated as well (Woodrow, 2001). Broad inclusion within the intellectual community, therefore, becomes paramount in developing intellectual and pedagogical paradigms. It is inappropriate to regard international openness as beginning and ending with reciprocity in terms of the content of ideas, sharing experience and a simple cultural relativism. It is far more important to recognize the role of cognitive reciprocity and to include within our pedagogical and intellectual understanding an openness to different ways of thinking, knowing and understanding those processes.

Conclusion: cultural practices and institutional challenges

What emerges from the discussion in this chapter is an indication of some of the basic intellectual paradoxes inherent within contemporary HE internationalization. Institutionally, universities exist within educational and intellectual environments that are emphatically local in their prevailing sense of identity and embedded within their routine practices, values and beliefs. At the same time, not only in response to recent economic globalization, universities exist as cross-border entities and are enlivened by the international nature of the intellectual traffic that flows between them. Particularly within the context of historically successful imperial societies, the temptations of conceptual colonialism are seductive because of the highly implicit nature of much that underlies routine educational practices. Yet the continued implicit privileging of the local can engender intellectual and educational redundancy because of its reliance upon historical rather than contemporary reference points. For HEIs both experiencing and aspiring to internationalize, therefore, it is essential to develop practices that not only capture the contemporary *Zeitgeist* but also are capable of responding to the continuing dynamic interplay of international intellectual and social forces. To do so inevitably involves the profound disruption of pre-existing institutional psycho-social identities and requires a major reassessment both of practices and beliefs. In a management sense, therefore, one of the key challenges inherent within any shift towards more inclusive conceptions of internationalization must begin with making existing local values and practices more explicit. Notions of organizational change, as a process of complex personal and organizational learning, are well established (Argyris and Schon, 1978, 1992). Inevitably, however, the quantum change implied by Transformative internationalization is significant.

We will discuss strategic management issues in more detail in Chapter 7. As a starting point in the process, it seems essential to undertake some kind of institutional cultural audit, however, such as that indicated in Chapter 2. Such an audit has the potential to provide a means of exploring how far routine organizational systems and practices embed local cultural assumptions about the purpose and practice of HE and the degree to which those local norms are valid, informed and consistent within the institution's operations. In large part this is a matter of exploring and capturing the kinds of fundamentals discussed in this chapter. Such an exercise certainly does not imply the inevitable abandonment of established local practices. Any institutional change exercise aimed at improving accessibility, however, must begin with the need to make existing values transparent and to evaluate the extent to which operational systems and infrastructure support or contradict them. An essential part of such an evaluation necessarily involves the articulation of the institutional orientation towards internationalization, indicating whether the strategic aim is to make local practices accessible to diverse participants in the institution or to re-evaluate the institutional posture, attempting to capture the international in its values and practices more explicitly.

Chapter 4

International students

Educational globalization for students

In Chapter 1 we discussed a key concern of this text that the internationalization of HEIs in Anglophone countries requires a process of development of institutional systems and practices to create an internationally integrated community. We follow the earlier discussion on institutional orientations towards internationalization with an exploration of how these orientations influence local institutional cultures and practices and the quality of the student experience. This chapter focuses on educational globalization for students. It explores the ways in which the international student is constructed in the academic practice literature and in the perceptions of key staff in HEIs. We contrast discussions about the need to accommodate cross-border students/differences in local university classrooms with a broader conception of student diversity and with the aims of 'Internationalization at Home' (Teekens, 2005).

Globalization has been described as 'the cross-national flow of goods, production and technology' (Jeong-eun Rhee and Sagaria, 2004, p. 78). Within this definition educational globalization can be construed as the cross-national flow of knowledge, awards, ideas, experiences and competences. International students have been described as 'the new global generation' (Rizvi, 2000, cited in Jeong-eun Rhee and Sagaria, 2004, p. 79) moving across countries and continents to pursue their interests and prepare for life and work in an interdependent world. The flow of students during the 1990s was predominantly from the third world to the first, and this one-way flow has been associated with discussions about power relations and Western intellectual colonization and imperialism (Burbules and Torres, 2000, cited in Jeong-eun Rhee and Sagaria, 2004, p. 80).

In contrast to these 'unequal cultural and intellectual exchanges'(Jeong-eun Rhee and Sagaria, 2004, p. 81), a more inclusive definition of 'the international student' is emerging, which emphasizes the reciprocal development of intercultural competences and global skills. The shift towards a competence-based approach to internationalization has implications for overseas students, indigenous and other domestic students, and the staff who work with them, as they engage in a process of exploring and understanding the cultural values that underpin their expectations of teaching and learning.

In inclusive settings, there is an obligation to identify and make explicit the prevailing culture at the HEI, to explicitly discuss the rationale for the structure and practices of learning and teaching in the institution, and to explore differences in cultural knowledge traditions with students (Schroder, 2001). The chapter concludes with an assessment of the key implications for academic practitioners, their work, identities, and professional development needs as we move towards an inclusive approach.

The new international student

Student and academic mobility continue to make a significant contribution to the economic and intellectual resources of HEIs. In a survey by the American Council on Education (ACE, 2000), the majority of the public thought that higher education students should have an overseas experience while studying and regarded knowledge about international issues as an important aspect of study and employability.

International experience is recognized as both personally desirable and as a useful addition to the curriculum vitae. Students may be motivated to study abroad by a desire to travel, to meet new people and to experience other cultures, and by aspirations and intentions to develop language skills, intercultural competencies and global awareness in order to enhance their career prospects (Milstein, 2005). Hence constructions in much of the literature of the international student involve mobility and study abroad. It is unsurprising therefore that the internationalization process in many universities has tended to focus predominantly on growth in cross-border student flows (Humfrey, 1999; Mortimer, 1997; Robson and Turner, 2007).

With greater government, employer and public focus on the benefits of study abroad, the climate for international study is favourable, yet the uptake of opportunities in a range of countries is conservative. Hamilton (1998, cited in Clyne and Rizvi, 1998) found that only 0.2 per cent of all Australian university students participated in exchange programmes. Less than 1 per cent of American HE students study abroad each year, and only 8 per cent of students study a foreign language at the tertiary level (Fantini *et al.*, 2001, cited in Daly and

Barker, 2005). Similarly, less than 1 per cent of Canadian university students study abroad as part of their degree (Knight, 2000, cited in Fantini *et al.*, 2001), whereas in Europe around 5 per cent of undergraduate students participate in exchange programmes annually (Teichler and Jahr, 2001, cited in Daly and Barker, 2005). For the majority of these students international mobility will involve a short-term experience overseas in an exchange, study tour, conference, visit, clinical placement, or work experience of around 1 to 6 weeks (Back, Davis and Olsen, 1996; Australian International Education Foundation, 1998).

The slightly higher participation rates in study abroad evident in Europe may be partly attributed to the extensive financial support available to students within the European Union (deWit, 1995). In the 20 years since its inception, well over a million students have taken part in the Erasmus mobility programme and the 2007 launch by the European Commission (EC) of the new Lifelong Learning Programme aims to mobilize a further 3 million students by 2012.

The Bologna Process has been agreed across EU states with the intention to create a European Higher Education Area by 2010, with student and staff mobility as a priority. Many European countries have engaged in a process of modernization, extensively restructuring HE to respond to the challenges of globalization and to promote employability (Gatfield, 1997; Clyne and Rizvi, 1998; Fantini *et al.*, 2001). Differences in HE systems and qualifications are being addressed to make the length, content, structure, quality and assessment of programmes more consistent and compatible, with an emphasis on competencies and flexible learning pathways. Students are faced with an ever-increasing choice of units or programmes from a range of institutions that can be accredited under common recognition procedures within the bachelor, master's and doctoral cycle.

The UK still has some way to go to comply with the Bologna obligations and falls significantly behind France, Spain, Germany and Italy in numbers of students participating in overseas study opportunities (*Education Guardian*, 2006). While there has been an expansion of possibilities for partnerships between universities in the UK and other countries for flexible course delivery, the growth in the numbers of European countries offering English-medium courses poses both opportunities and threats to UK HEIs.

Meanwhile the steady flow to the UK and US of students from more distant markets, principally East Asian countries, will inevitably diminish with the growth of HE in those countries, as domestic universities expand their postgraduate provision. Singapore and

Malaysia, for example, have positioned themselves as education hubs
to attract international students (*Education Guardian*, 2006).

Despite the competitive market, Mazzarol and Soutar (2002, cited
in Lord and Dawson, 2003) found that the reputation of Anglophone
universities remains high. This has opened up opportunities for
international providers to establish offshore campuses and distance-
learning options. Student perceptions of Anglophone universities have
a powerful influence on recruitment, influenced by a range of factors
related to the nature and range of programmes on offer, the marketing
approach of the university and discipline, the international standing
of the university and the personal recommendations of friends, family
or sponsors. Ninety-three per cent of Indian respondents perceived
overseas courses to be better than courses delivered in their own
country. Chinese and Indian participants perceived UK qualifications
to be more highly regarded in their respective home countries than
Australian qualifications (Lord and Dawson, 2003).

Many Southeast Asian students are motivated to travel to Western
countries for higher education as a way to acquire 'western credentials
and expertise because these [are perceived to] offer workplace
flexibility and geographic mobility' (Singh and Docherty, 2004, p.
10). This perception is based on the experience of graduates who have
returned from study in Anglophone universities to successful careers
and senior positions in their own countries. When international
students 'voluntarily reconstitute their identities across national
borders' to engage with Western political, economic and intellectual
exchange as 'consenting participants', this neutralizes the power
differential and imperialist arguments (Jeong-eun Rhee and Sagaria,
2004, p. 91)

However, the UK HE sector has been criticized for complacency in
working with international students, and reliance on its educational
reputation (British Council, Educational Counselling Service,
2000). The literature provides numerous examples of the difficulties
encountered by international students upon arrival in the host country,
related to culture shock, understanding and adaptation to learning and
teaching conventions, and integration into the host community (Tsui,
1996, cited in Cheng, 2000; Flowerdew and Miller, 1995; Watkins
and Biggs, 1996, cited in Cruickshank, 2004).

The dichotomies between the Asian and Anglophone systems and
attitudes in Chapter 3 highlighted the potential challenges for Asian
students studying in the UK, when HEIs retain the local cultural and
the learning traditions that have been developed around the needs
of the archetypal British student. The Anglo/Asian dichotomy is
only part of the challenge: other culturally based learning traditions

and experiences are represented as British universities play host to increasingly diverse populations. Ritchie (2006) identified students from over 100 countries at one institution in 2003–4, representing 15 per cent of the total student population. Many other university websites boast similar claims to diversity. With shifting markets HEIs cannot afford to be complacent: understanding diverse student motivations and educational expectations and responding appropriately to students' support requirements is essential to an academically and socially inclusive environment and a high-quality student experience.

The international student experience: integrating international and intercultural goals

From a somewhat piecemeal attempt at internationalization consisting 'of a series of disconnected activities that are weakly integrated into the core academic mission' (Green, 2003, p. 16), internationalization has begun to occupy a more central position in university strategic discussions, largely driven by the impetus to focus on the provision of high-quality experiences to international students. Attention is drawn to the important question of how institutions 'deal with the intersection of international and intercultural' (Knight, 2004, p. 49) as they reassess the purposes, processes and practices of higher education (De Vita and Case, 2003; Gibbs and Simpson, 2004).

This brings strategic discussions around internationalization closer to issues concerning 'domestic' ethnic and cultural diversity. Common goals of international and diversity policies are designed to prepare students for careers in the global economy and to facilitate greater intercultural understanding, tolerance and respect (Black, 2004; Caruana and Hanstock, 2005). Increasingly HEIs seek to achieve these goals by providing students with opportunities to acquire new competencies and experiences overseas or by enriching the wider student experience at home by integrating the knowledge and experience of international and ethnic minority students and other domestic students (Stier, 2002, cited in Caruana and Hanstock, 2005). Addressing how the learning experience of domestic students can be enriched by a more internationalized approach, so-called Internationalization at Home, is an important aspect of the internationalization process.

The increasing student diversity within university settings provides opportunities for all students to develop intercultural skills. However, simply placing diverse groups of learners together does not guarantee that intercultural learning will take place (Teekens, 2003; Otten, 2003; Bennett, 1993). The increased integration of internationalization policies with diversity policies presents challenges for curriculum development and skill changes to equip students to work in a global economy and assist HEIs to maintain a competitive position in the increasingly global educational marketplace (Stier, 2003).

Global skills and competencies

In discussing the internationalization of higher education institutions in Japan, Aoki (2005) adopts Soderqvist's (2002, p. 29) definition of internationalization as:

> . . . a change process from a national higher education institution to an international higher education institution leading to the inclusion of an international dimension in all aspects of its holistic management in order to enhance the quality of teaching and learning and to achieve the desired competencies. (Soderqvist, 2002, p. 29)

In the globalizing marketplace, employers are increasingly seeking graduates with skills and characteristics that enable them to be more competitive in the international arena (Industry Task Force on Leadership and Management Skills, 1995). Institutions are liaising with employers internationally to identify more precisely the skills and qualities required for work in the international context (see Figure 4.1), and underpin programme objectives with the requirement that students rehearse and acquire international business knowledge and skills and intercultural awareness and competencies (Moses, 2003; Waghid, 2002; Webb *et al.*, 1999; Australian International Education Foundation, 1998; Fantini *et al.*, 2001; *Education Guardian*, 2006).

Enabling graduates to acquire global competencies and cultural intelligence requires consideration of the employability, cognitive, attitudinal and intercultural dimensions of their university experience and the interactional aspects of dealing with people from different contexts, ethnicities and languages (Knight, 1999; Leask, 2001). Curricula with defined objectives to integrate intercultural learning can promote recognition of the ways in which cultural factors and practices influence diverse understandings as individuals seek relevance and meaning in their world (Teekens, 2003; Paige and Mestenhauser, 1999; Paige, 2003; Caruana and Hanstock, 2005).

Figure 4.1: Global skills. Adapted from the Newcastle University Global Skills blueprint (www.careers.ncl.ac.uk/cu/sis_global_skills.php)

Employability skills	Definition
Self-knowledge and reflection	Engaging in reflective activities to assist self-knowledge, and understanding the values, qualities and skills required for personal and professional development
Planning and organizing	**Setting objectives, planning actions and managing time and resources effectively in order to achieve personal and organizational goals**
1 Goal setting and action planning	Setting objectives, scheduling resources and managing time
2 Decision making	Being aware of and choosing between opportunities/ solutions that achieve goals, having gathered and evaluated relevant information
Personal enterprise	**Respond to opportunities and initiate change for continuous improvement**
1 Creativity	Generating and visualizing new ideas and concepts
2 Initiative	Identifying and making effective use of material, financial and human resources
3 Adaptability	Responding readily to changing situations and priorities
4 Problem-solving	Critically evaluating complex information and identifying key issues for action
Communication	**Effectively use of speech, writing, technology and behaviour in order to present and exchange opinions, ideas and information**
1 Oral	Using spoken language appropriate to the context and the purpose
2 Interpersonal	Using and responding to non-verbal behaviour, including active listening techniques
3 Written/other	Using written and other appropriate tools and resources to support and enhance other forms of communication
Team working	**Working with others in order to establish and achieve common goals**
1 Collaboration	Recognizing and making best use of the knowledge, values, qualities and skills of individuals
2 Relationship-building	Creating and maintaining an environment in which risks and rewards are shared by all
3 Leadership	Establishing direction, winning the commitment of others and taking responsibility for actions and decisions

An integrated programme of course work, cross-curricular events and community and cultural experiences can offer opportunities to apply skills and knowledge, and develop understandings of the complex cultural issues at play in work, community and public life. This might include an experience abroad, a practicum or project in a local ethnic or immigrant community, or involvement in extracurricular multicultural and international events either on campus or in the local community (Mason and Stanley, 1997).

Positive outcomes for individual students, such as the development of greater global awareness, concern and interest, enhanced self-awareness and more critical attitudes toward one's own country are cited by Milstein (2005) as potential benefits related to students' international experiences. Enhanced intercultural awareness is also important for tutors, managers and administrators in Anglophone HEIs in order to promote understanding of students' needs and the ways in which earlier learning experiences influence students' behaviour and development as learners in their new context (Turner and Acker, 2002).

Developing intercultural understanding and reducing barriers to learning

As we discussed in the previous chapter, implicit cultural influences have a significant impact on student learning behaviours and expectations and adjustment in new learning situations. While wishing to avoid stereotypical constructions of students from particular contexts, we thought it important to consider the cultural factors that have gained attention in the literature in relation to student adjustment. Much of the literature relates to the problems that may arise when Asian students embark on studies in Anglophone universities. East Asian students in particular have been characterized as passive or unquestioning learners who find speaking in Western academic settings challenging, particularly when required to make oral presentations (Braddock *et al.*, 1995; Cortazzi and Jin, 1996; Felix, 1992, cited in Adams, 2004).

Similarly, Western teachers working in Asian universities have found students to be shy, passive, diligent, very good at memorization, but unwilling to work in groups, and not comfortable with critical thinking (Chan and Droyer, 1996, cited in Turner and Acker, 2002; Tsui, 1996, cited in Cheng, 2000; Flowerdew and Miller, 1995). Students' apparent reticence about participation in class and preference for traditional lecture input has been attributed to a desire not to stand out, as cultural values of collectivism promote the desire to maintain harmony within the group rather than individual self-expression (Flowerdew and Miller, 1995).

The discussion in Chapter 3 illustrates that respect for the authority and expertise of the teacher may also inhibit student engagement in the problem-oriented argument and discussion and interactive teaching strategies that are encouraged in Anglophone universities to promote deep transformational learning (Harman, 2003). Thus a highly deferential approach is often adopted by Chinese, Japanese and Korean students raised in conformist educational cultures. This does not preclude a more personal connection and social relationship outside the classroom. In the Hindu educational tradition, the teacher or learned person is expected to attend to the holistic needs of the student, and provide spiritual, moral and intellectual guidance (Chan and Droyer, 1996, cited in Turner and Acker, 2002; Tsui, 1996; cited in Cheng, 2000; Flowerdew and Miller, 1995).

However, the perception of the cultural influences reflected in these accounts has been challenged as exaggerated and over-generalized (Cheng, 2000; Zhou *et al.*, 2005). Cadman (2000) and Ramburuth and McCormick (2001) caution against a conceptualization of all international students as unquestioning conduits for the transfer of skills and knowledge and suggest that relying on anecdotal evidence and generalized statements is unwise. Cheng (2000, p. 441) points out that the term for knowledge in Chinese is made up of two characters: *xue* = to learn and *wen* = to ask. Thus enquiring and questioning are important in the quest for knowledge and assumptions that Asian students are uncomfortable with critical approaches must be questioned. Claxton (1996a, cited in Turner and Acker, 2002, p. 167) proposes that it may be more appropriate to investigate the learners' implicit theories of learning.

Zhou *et al.* (2005, p.307) suggest that an

appreciation of diversity in the classroom requires the open exchange of ideas and experiences of students from different backgrounds. However, the content of these exchanges and the extent to which knowledge (including indigenous knowledge) is shared may be compromised in the classroom setting.

Factors that influence students' level of participation include proficiency in communication and a wide range of other elements related to cultural familiarity with the learning methods and the power differential between languages, cultures and knowledges in the setting.

Ramburuth and McCormick (2001) investigated the differences between domestic (Australian) and international students in their approaches to learning and found differences in students' use of surface strategies, but no significant differences in their deep approaches to learning (Marton and Säljö, 1976). This suggests that perceptions about the rote learning behaviours of international students are unhelpful and that it may be more fruitful to investigate situational factors influencing their apparent reticence in Western learning environments. These may be related to unfamiliar teaching methodologies, such as teacher-centred methodology, or to irrelevant or offensive topics, a lack of rapport between teacher and students, or the context- or discipline-specific language that is used.

The challenges of adjustment to the learning norms of the Anglophone institution may be more acute for students from traditional Eastern cultures, although Western influences may have penetrated students' earlier learning experiences, particularly when they have studied in a major city or had access to advanced media and technology. However, European Union (EU) students also encounter a series of challenges and support needs as they adjust to the language, cultural and social context, and the academic standards and expectations of the host university (Biggs, 1999, cited in Bamford *et al.*, 2002). Adjustment will depend on the extent to which the cognitive, affective and situational aspects of learning, together with the many other factors impacting on students' experiences of living in the host country, complement or conflict with their expectations (Claxton, 1996a; Adams, 2004; Busher, 2001, cited in Leonard and Morley, 2003). This turns attention to the need for innovative strategies for diversity management and highlights the importance of academic orientation for students and targeted resources to support curriculum and pedagogical development and cross-cultural awareness for staff (Ramburuth and McCormick, 2001).

Student expectations and the institutional culture

Student expectations of the study programme and the ease with which they become accustomed to the norms of the institution, both in terms of the overall culture and the specific learning environment in which they operate, will be influenced by their educational and personal histories and experiences, achievements, social backgrounds and gender (Pascarella and Terenzini, 2005, cited in Richardson and Edmunds, 2007; Lord and Dawson, 2003). Learning may be inhibited when students don't have a clear understanding of the discursive nature of learning, the rules of turn-taking, paired work or group work and the assessment criteria and the rules of authorship in the host university (Cheng, 2000).

Language competence is an important prerequisite for a successful academic experience. Second- or third- language proficiency is important to intercultural competence, enabling students to transcend their native language, culture and world-view to communicate effectively in other cultures (Daly and Barker, 2005; Stephens, 1997; Hellsten and Prescott, 2004). The language requirements for university study, measured for example through the Test of English as a Foreign Language (TOEFL) or the International English Language Testing System (IELTS), are designed to assess the ability of non-native speakers to use and understand English as it is spoken and written in academic settings, but will not ensure a level of language proficiency for more sophisticated engagement or the expression of ideas (Cheng, 2000).

Culturally specific language and learning tools are important components of students' individual identities (Sanchez, 2000; Berger, 2000). Erlenawati (2005) notes that the traditional approach to EFL pedagogies in Asia, and East Asia in particular, focuses mainly on learning to read and preparation for assignment writing. There is little emphasis on conversational skills, hence students may be unprepared for the dialogic nature of classroom communication in Anglophone contexts (Holmes, 2004), whereas a communicative approach prepares students for an expanded emphasis on oral communication.

Students' concerns about the perceived adequacy of their language styles and abilities will affect their confidence about speaking in public, and willingness to ask or answer questions in class or to make oral presentations (Mok *et al.*, 2001; Chalmers and Volet, 1997). Some universities have adopted more facilitative approaches where lecture notes and online materials are provided in a range of languages and student discussions and group work in the first language are encouraged. Stephens (1997) and Tomlinson and Dat (2004) found that Asian students freely and independently participated in discussion when they understood the ground rules for engagement. Understanding may be inhibited when the language used in lectures is vague, or culturally situated, as may be the case with the use of metaphor. Students who have not penetrated the situated language conventions of their discipline may be unintentionally excluded from the lecture, seminar or discussion.

Zhou *et al.* (2005) found that while improvements in English language skills and knowledge of Western culture assisted participation for some students, others chose to remain silent. This was attributed to contextual factors related to students' limited understanding of classroom discourses and academic practices (Zhou *et al.*, 2005). This suggests the value of acculturation strategies within induction arrangements, to make explicit the norms and rules within the particular HEI while being sensitive to the power differential between different languages and cultures, e.g. the expectations of women coming to study in the West from patriarchal societies (Bada, 1994, cited in Leonard and Morley, 2001). The expectations for change in students' familiar learning and social behaviours, and the implications for readjustment when students return to their home countries, cannot be underestimated.

Moving towards a more culturally inclusive approach

Simply giving students more information to acculturate them into the host institution's 'way of doing things' is neither appropriate nor adequate (Wright, 1997; Cadman, 2000). While there are undoubtedly challenges as students adapt their learning behaviours, e.g. to learning independently if they are accustomed to structured learning situations, to move from reproductive to the more critical forms of thinking valued in western settings, implicit in these challenges is the inflexibility and superiority of Western traditions (Ballard, 1995, cited in Cadman, 2000).

Cadman's (2000) data demonstrate students' appreciation of a reciprocal learning approach: negotiating a common postgraduate culture enables students from different national cultures to communicate effectively. This has much wider implications for academic staff, who may be required to move out of their comfort zone and familiar ways of performing to develop more culturally sensitive modes of delivery and to review curriculum content to ensure that it represents international perspectives.

Cruickshank (2004) suggests the notion of cultural inclusiveness lies more in the willingness to negotiate learning and teaching strategies than in the adoption of any specific approach to pedagogy. Understanding and acceptance by faculty and peers of students' knowledge traditions is important to the individual's sense of value and competence. Where there are reciprocal adjustments in instructional approaches, classroom management, curriculum content and resources, many students have a positive and successful learning experience (Humfrey, 1999; Littlemore, 2001). This refocuses discussions on teaching practices to facilitate learning access for all participants (Robson and Turner, 2007; Biggs, 1999; Moseley *et al.*,

2004) based upon thought-through pedagogies, made transparent and accessible for different student communities.

Organizational mediation occurs through the organization of the curriculum and practical issues concerning staff, students, time and place (Richardson and Edmunds, 2007). This extends the discussion of learning outcomes beyond notions of competence, skill and particular cultural bodies of knowledge towards questions of personal identity, confidence, citizenship and social values. Learning for each individual student is shaped by experiences in their first culture and any additional cultures they may encounter. Students have opportunities and choices to resist, subvert or challenge the cultural practices to which they are exposed (Teekens, 2005; Liddicoat, 2004, cited in Caruana and Hanstock, 2005). Learning is enhanced in the host culture when both the activities and outcomes have meaning for all participants (Pascarella and Terenzini, 2005). This wider-ranging and more inclusive focus on individual learner experiences, needs and identities requires a cultural shift in the institution to mainstream international students into the academic and social life of the university, while at the same time ensuring sensitivity to cultural differences.

Pettigrew and Tropp (2000, p. 11) suggest that 'optimal contact situations' can be created to develop intercultural competence as an essential outcome for all participants, whether international or domestic students, faculty or staff. The active engagement of learners from different cultural backgrounds in collaborative learning tasks or experiences can improve international or intercultural knowledge, skills and attitudes that promote inclusion and respect for all learners (Whalley, 2001).

While the increasing student diversity within university settings provides opportunities for all students to develop intercultural skills and understanding, respect and tolerance (International Association of Universities, cited in Black, 2004), domestic and international students may not readily interact, and may maintain a rather distant and superficial relationship (Ward and Masgoret, 2004; Daly and Barker, 2005). Ward and Masgoret (2004) recommended that studies of domestic students' and host communities' perceptions of international students should be conducted and that programmes designed to enhance the relationships between domestic and international students and between international students and members of the wider community should be initiated and evaluated. Measures to improve relations and improve the frequency and quality of intercultural contact between international and host students are important (Ward and Masgoret, 2004). Social interactions, i.e. the number and quality of relationships an international student has with host country nationals, has been positively linked to satisfaction and adjustment for international students (Adrian-Taylor *et al.*, 2007).

Implications for academic practitioners: moving towards a culturally inclusive pedagogy

We have explored constructions of 'the international student' as multi-ethnic and multi-lingual students; incoming international (and European) students; outgoing study abroad or exchange students; and ethnically diverse 'home' populations, whose university experience is enriched by the introduction of international, intercultural and global dimensions into the curriculum and a more culturally inclusive approach to learning (Daly and Barker, 2005; Knight, 2004; Aoki, 2005). Rather than focusing on internationalization as a competitive response to a financial imperative (recruiting increasing numbers of international students to keep HE institutions afloat), a broader focus on developing global culture, perspectives and identities for students and faculty offers more promise for qualitative institutional improvement.

Intercultural competence is an increasingly important professional attribute and, as such, can be viewed as an important outcome for all graduates, to prepare them for a global economy and society. Bennett and Bennett (2004) define intercultural competence in terms of a mindset and a skillset. An intercultural mindset involves awareness of operating in a cultural context and conscious knowledge of one's own culture (cultural self-awareness) and of frameworks for comparison of cultural contrasts (e.g. communication styles, cultural values). This useful conceptualization moves beyond the much criticized skills and competences approaches to describe a metacognitive model in which individuals develop an ability to analyse interaction, predict misunderstanding, adapt behaviours in different cultural settings and develop an understanding about the cultural characteristics of others that avoids stereotyping.

If the aim of internationalization is to transform the cultural community, the discourses and the learning environment at HEIs (Williams, 2005), there are challenges to the working practices of all staff across the institution. This may involve a level of discomfort as the institutional imperative to internationalize dislodges individuals from familiar ways of doing things, prevailing pedagogies and modes of delivery (De Vita and Case, 2003).

One of the challenges for professional development is to narrow the gap between the expectations of students and academic staff by working towards a synergy of educational cultures (Kingston and Forland, 2004). This requires a mutual effort by all participants to learn about, understand and appreciate each others' cultures, to be open to alternative interpretations of learning and reciprocity, and to learn with and from others (Jin and Cortazzi, 2002, p. 1). Increasing the range of discursive opportunities for staff and students to share their experiences of internationalization assists professionals to reflect on their practice, enhances awareness of their roles in relation to students and colleagues, and improves understanding of their own and others' expectations, assumptions, ethics and values (Robson and Turner, 2007; Bolton, 2005, p. 272).

When lecturers' and students' conceptions of learning are similar, it is less likely that students will experience difficulties in learning (Newton, 2000). Reflective discussions can support conceptual change and a broader vision of internationalization and promote the development of culturally inclusive pedagogies and practices (Causey *et al.*, 1999). Where a dialogue takes place between students and tutors or supervisors, to reflect upon the models of understanding which underpin student learning behaviour and guide teachers' work, this can lead to reciprocal adjustment in instructional approaches, settings, curriculum content and resources (Newton, 2000; Ho *et al.*, 2001). This shifts the focus from the need to adapt provision for international students to a reconceptualization of learning and teaching in postgraduate studies with potential benefits for other students, including mature students who have not engaged in formal education for some years, or non-traditional learners (Leonard and Morley, 2003).

In reflective discussion, 'the narratives and metaphors by which we structure our lives, the taken-for-granteds, are questioned and challenged' (Bolton, 2005, p. 274). Explanations or narratives are created, which enhance awareness and understanding of the circumstances and situations in which individuals operate. The tacit rules of well-established discourse communities (the discourse of the internationalization, for example, or the discourse of assessment) are explored and renegotiated with new members of the community (Williams, 2005). Addressing fears about change in a positive and constructive manner and assisting established and new participants to explore and optimize the match between their theories of teaching and learning and those required in an internationalized institution can help to foster an overall positive cultural climate.

Canning (2007) introduces the notion of pedagogy as a discipline with a culture and identity that is constructed as the broader environment of HE as it impacts upon the interactions between learners, teachers and knowledge. Critical pedagogy as a discipline in HE is nurtured by reflection on practice and debates about the nature of HE and the practices of teaching and learning (Canning, 2007).

Central initiatives in professional development related to cross-cultural issues and working with diversity that incorporate reflective practice, action research, networks or study groups, or engage tutors in the kinds of learning that they are expected to provide for their students, have been found to impact positively on practice (Ho *et al.*, 2001; Boyle *et al.*, 2004). Conceptual change requires longer-term engagement in the kind of professional development that encourage participants to clarify their personal conceptions of internationalization and its impact on learning and teaching, to enhance awareness of student needs and confront inadequacies or gaps in existing conceptions and pedagogies (Ho *et al.*, 2001; Boyle *et al.*, 2004).

We will discuss further the impact of internationalization on curriculum, teaching and assessment in Chapter 5 and undertake a more detailed analysis of the challenges it presents for academic development in Chapter 8.

Chapter 5

International curriculum, teaching and assessment

This chapter addresses the key teaching practice implications arising from internationalization, with the challenges of classroom diversity and the shift from monocultural to multicultural groups. The chapter discusses the contribution of social and cultural learning to the development of intercultural competences, explores issues around intercultural group working and cooperation, styles of participation and the development of inclusive practices. A case study illustrates the implicit teaching and learning conventions in a UK university and identifies the challenges presented to prevailing work patterns and identities as perceived by staff working with increasingly diverse cohorts of cross-border and non-traditional students. The chapter concludes with a range of suggestions for inclusive academic experiences and assessment practices.

The challenges of classroom diversity

In the previous chapter we examined some of the characterizations of international students in the literature and the challenges faced by many students as they confront Western academic and cultural expectations (Bayley *et al.*, 2002; Borland and Pearce, 2002; Mulligan and Kirkpatrick, 2000; Hellsten, 2002; Wong, 2004; Adams, 2004; Cadman, 2000). The dominant discourse appears to centre on what universities do to fit international students into their existing cultures and on the problems created by assimilation models in which the 'necessary adjustments [are] made primarily by the incoming postgraduates, often with very little reciprocal adjustment' (Cadman, 2000, pp. 476–7).

McTaggart (2003) draws attention to the necessity for two kinds of institutional response, in order to make the curriculum more relevant and engaging for students from a range of cultures and to help to prepare domestic and international students to live and work in settings and organizations that differ from the host culture.

HE institutions are therefore attempting to find ways 'to educate from, with, and for a multitude of cultural perspectives' (Nainby, Warren and Bollinger, 2003, p. 198, cited in Bretag, 2006). Internationalization has also been associated with the development of civic responsibilities and democratic principles, aiming to develop graduates who will lead productive working lives, both locally and globally (Green and Olsen, 2003). In democratic learning situations, McTaggart (2003, p. 2) refers to 'relational participation', which embodies inclusive practices, where teachers and students negotiate the curriculum, consider the relationships between the Western cultural practices embedded in the curriculum and in students' own cultural practices, and in the intended work settings of those students.

By integrating an international or global dimension into the purpose, functions or delivery of programmes, universities can work towards a more inclusive climate (Knight, 2004). This requires the development of intercultural awareness and sensitivity in staff and home students as much as the adaptation of incoming students to Western forms of content delivery and knowledge creation. Some studies have demonstrated positive influences on student outcomes where institutions have found ways to respond to students' knowledge traditions, learning style preferences, motivations and learning strategies (Thomas, 2002; Sanchez, 2000; Szelenyi, 2001).

Understanding has increased of the ways in which the intercultural, professional, social and emotional dimensions of the curriculum can contribute to students' knowledge base and aptitude for life in multicultural contexts (Wachter, 2003; Whalley, 1997; Bell, 2005; Nilsson, 2000), developing flexible and occupationally versatile individuals, with 'cosmopolitan dispositions' (Bremer and van der Wende, 1995, cited in Caruana, 2004) who are willing to move beyond their traditional communities to update their skills (Morgan and Cohen, 2006; Harris, 2003).

International curriculum

International curricula have been defined as:

> Curricula with an international orientation in content, aimed at preparing students to perform (professionally/socially) in an international and multicultural context, and designed for domestic students as well as foreign students. (IDP, 1995, p. 1).

Internationalizing the curriculum will involve reviewing the content (contexts, values and understandings), the processes of teaching and learning and assessment, and the skills required for life and work in a diverse world. Leask (1999, p. 3) supports this view, describing internationalization as 'the implementation of a range of teaching processes designed to assist all students to learn about and understand the international context of their studies, and to operate effectively in international professional environments'.

International issues have long been integral to specific disciplines and curricula, for example in cultural anthropology, comparative religion and philosophy, political science or social geography (Caruana and Hanstock, 2005). More recently the development of courses with an international and/or multicultural dimension to the subject area have been designed to promote the knowledge and professional skills graduates will need to work or study in a global economy. Curricula with international subject matter such as language studies, or linguistics, which address cross-cultural communication issues, and curricula leading to joint or combined degrees, for example international marketing within international business management, or cross-cultural communication themes in combination with law, education or media studies, have gained popularity and promote awareness of the cultural factors that influence diverse understandings (Teekens, 2003; Paige and Mestenhauser, 1999; Paige, 2003; IDP, 1995).

Positive effects such as increased knowledge of the international theoretical or practical elements of the discipline, enhanced understanding and ability to communicate with people from other countries (including improved foreign language proficiency), and improved social and cultural integration of diverse student groups have been reported where intercultural, interdisciplinary and comparative perspectives have been infused into the curriculum and integrated approaches to developing content, teaching and learning strategies, instructional materials and resources, assessment strategies and support mechanisms have been adopted (Ellingboe, 1998; Teekens, 2003; Nilsson, 2000; Otten, 2000). While this may not be appropriate in every area of a programme, arguably each degree programme should incorporate an international dimension. Many European universities have begun to integrate mandatory courses on international and intercultural issues in study programmes across a range of disciplines to develop students' 'intercultural competence, critical thinking and comparative thinking' (Yershova *et al.*, 2000, cited in Otten, 2003, pp. 18–19). Programmes that aim to be culturally inclusive can progressively develop ways to assess intercultural skills and inclusive, open, and reflective behaviours (Mezirow, 2000).

Language, culture and knowledge construction

The intercultural dimension of the HE experience can also develop students' ability to contribute to the intercultural construction, exchange and use of knowledge (Odgers and Giroux, 2006). Rizvi (2000, p. 2) argues that workplace changes now require high levels of cognitive and communication skills. As we discussed in the previous chapter, knowledge is culturally situated and the narratives that are created to exchange knowledge are closely tied to particular institutional and cultural norms (Gilbert, 2005) and communities of learning. Learning is dependent on the construction of discipline knowledge through the use of language and concepts which are often culturally nuanced (Scarino *et al.*, 2005). Consideration of the relevance of curriculum content to the intended audience, and how the cognitive abilities required for participants to successfully interact with the curriculum are implicitly and explicitly negotiated, is therefore important.

Students' academic and intercultural literacy skills are developed within disciplinary discourses which mediate knowledge through established ways of using and understanding language (Scarino *et al.*, 2005). Simply placing diverse groups of learners together does not guarantee that intercultural learning will take place (Teekens, 2003; Otten, 2003; Bennett, 1993). The mediation of intercultural learning requires conscious reflection on individual and planned opportunities for social learning experiences with people from other cultures rather than simply co-locating students for classes (Otten, 2003). This process takes time, particularly for students learning in a second or third language (Scarino *et al.*, 2005). Students may be disadvantaged if they are not inducted into the discourse, or if the expectations within the social learning context conflict with their prior assumptions about what is appropriate in such situations. This may apply to 'minority' indigenous groups as well as 'international' students (Marshall and Martin, 2000; Asmar, 2001).

Curriculum delivery methods commonly used in Anglophone countries may prove challenging for students who have previously studied in cultural settings where more traditional and didactic methods are employed. Approaches that embody democratic or constructivist principles and incorporate group work or oral presentations may create anxiety (Bruner, 1996; Barnett, 1997). Otten (2000) suggests that attention should be directed to the relative social positions of lecturers and students in different cultures and how the expected patterns of student-student and tutor-student interactions in the HEI setting influence learning. Passive responses can be misinterpreted as indicative of limitations in students' intellectual ability (Asmar, 2004; Stoicovy, 2002), when in many instances students' sense of competence with regard to their English language proficiency has been found to be the principal barrier to learning (Wong, 2004; Hellsten and Prescott, 2004). Students accustomed to teacher-centred forms of learning, often with a strong focus on grammar and correct usage, may find it difficult to make the transition to more independent and interactive forms of learning (Hellsten, 2002).

While caution must be exercised about making generic statements concerning international students (Erlenawati, 2005), Adams (2004, p. 116) cites data from surveys in Australian, Canadian and American universities that demonstrate that lack of confidence with oral skills is common in non-native speaking students and may lead to negative effects on self-confidence and learning outcomes. This highlights the importance of providing appropriate language support during the study period.

The development of culturally sensitive institutional responses with respect to students' cultural capital and learning expectations is also important in order that they can be 'fish in water' and learn well (Thomas, 2002, p. 431). Whereas study skills and language training may be necessary forms of support, they denote 'otherness', whereas cultural inclusivity reflects a more reciprocal individual and collective values-based stance (McTaggart, 2003, p. 8). Assisting students to become aware of their world-view requires a realization that one understands in a particular cultural way in order to find 'one's own "meaning-making" meaningful' (Bennett, 1993, p. 25) and a level of independence and autonomy to recognize and seek appropriate support where required. This leads to thinking at a meta-level.

A range of models and frameworks have been developed to try to describe and guide successful thinking and meta-cognitive learning. These can be useful to describe, guide and negotiate the sorts of thinking students are expected to demonstrate in classroom interactions and assessed work. Moseley *et al.* (2004) found that cognitive approaches emphasize particular mental processes, such as analysis, evaluation, inference, explanation and self-regulation (Pintrich, 2000; Anderson *et al.*, 2001). Philosophical interpretations have emphasized values and 'good thinking' (Ennis, 1985; Lipman, 2003), and the importance of a disposition to self-examine and self-correct (Moseley *et al.*, 2004; Facione, 1990), and to present one's position honestly, to 'get it right' (Ennis, 1985, p. 45). HEIs in many Anglophone countries make explicit the expectation for skills development, for example the cognitive skills and critical thinking skills that students are required to demonstrate in their work. The conative and affective dimensions of learning may be less clearly articulated and understood.

While existing frameworks give unequal weight to the cognitive, emotional and social dimensions of learning (Illeris, 2002), the Integrated Framework (Figure 5.1: Moseley *et al.*, 2004) was developed to incorporate the cognitive, conative and affective dimensions involved in engagement and value-grounded thinking, and in critical, creative and caring thinking, or emotional intelligence, described by Gardner (1983) as interpersonal and intrapersonal intelligence.

Figure 5.1: An extension of the Integrated Framework for understanding thinking and learning (Moseley et al., 2004)

Strategic and reflective thinking		
Engagement with and management of thinking and learning, supported by value-grounded thinking (including critically reflective thinking and interpersonal and intercultural sensitivity)		
Cognitive skills		
Information gathering	Building language and understanding	Productive thinking
Experiencing, recognizing and recalling		Reasoning
	Developing meaning (e.g. by elaborating, representing, organizing or sharing ideas)	Understanding causal relationships
Comprehending messages and recorded information		
		Systematic enquiry
	Understanding disciplinary discourses	Problem solving
	Working with patterns or rules	Creative thinking
		Intercultural awareness
	Concept formation	
	Developing intercultural skills and understanding through participation in knowledge cultures or communities of learning	

The framework may help curriculum designers to plan, describe and negotiate learning objectives and assist students to take control of planning their learning and performance with greater understanding of the expectations within the institution.

Studies have demonstrated positive influences on student outcomes where institutions attempt to make explicit the kinds of thinking and learning that are expected and respond to students' learning style preferences, motivations and learning strategies (Sanchez, 2000). Rizvi (2000) argues that curriculum approaches that seek to provide students with skills of inquiry and analysis and ability to think critically and reflect on knowledge, assist students to see its relevance and significance, usefulness and applicability. Self-efficacy can be enhanced by observing peer models of successful engagement with learning tasks (Adams, 2004).

Biggs' (1996) SOLO (Structure of the Observed Learning Outcome) taxonomy has also been found to be a useful foundation for assessment criteria in postgraduate professional development programmes in education (Moseley *et al.*, 2005) and in other settings as a framework for analysing learning objectives and tasks (Chan *et al.*, 2002). Biggs' (1996) notion of constructive alignment derives from the constructivist paradigm, which suggests that learners actively construct their own knowledge and understanding through reflection in context. In a constructively aligned teaching environment (Biggs, 1996), all stages of the process of curriculum design, delivery and assessment are planned to encourage student thinking and deepen levels of understanding. For example, understanding may be nominal if one or two aspects of a task are understood, but not in an integrated way. When all aspects of a task are understood in a coherent whole, relational thinking is possible. Higher levels of abstraction enable reconceptualization and generalization of learning to new situations or tasks. Individuals with an 'internationalized mindset' (Paige and Mestenhauser, 1999) effectively draw upon knowledge from diverse settings, cultures and languages, using skills to connect to, translate and synthesize cultural influences.

Achieving the level of sophisticated meta-cognitive skills required to underpin an internationalized mindset in teaching and learning (Paige and Mestenhauser, 1999) may require targeted staff development. The case study here illustrates the implicit teaching and learning conventions in one UK university and the challenges presented by internationalization as perceived by staff working with an increasingly diverse student population in one faculty.

Case study

This case study is set in a university which has recently undergone a radical restructure and is at a relatively early stage of internationalizing its activities. Approximately 40 per cent of postgraduate taught and research students at the institution are international. Senior managers began to set out an international strategy, to define what it might look like as an international university and how this might be achieved. They considered the implications for the academic community, including curriculum and skill changes to ensure a high-quality learning experience for international students. A cultural shift was needed, and it was recognized that this would be a long-term process. The vision for the future articulated by the senior management team highlighted internationalization as one of four major areas for growth. While activity inevitably focused predominantly on ways to increase recruitment, a university consultation paper indicated the emergence of a more holistic approach to internationalization in which the university was envisaged as an internationally minded community, not simply an institution with an increasingly large number of international students.

One of the three faculties in the institution reacted proactively to the increased central concern with internationalization by appointing the authors as International Teaching Fellows. This multi-disciplinary faculty hosted the largest number of international students in the university. Some schools had long and varied experience of international work, including offshore delivery, while others had only relatively recently experienced an influx of international students.

During the fellowships discussions took place with 35 (21 male: 14 female) key members of staff, including heads of schools, programme directors, senior administrators and lecturers who managed, supported and taught international students. The discussions explored what internationalization meant for individual roles and identities, reviewed support needs and, as one head of school put it, the cultural changes necessary to 'make the experience a quality experience for students'. Opportunities for discussion at a faculty awayday, a heads of schools' forum, in small, discipline-based group and one-to-one meetings were utilized over a two-year period to reveal individual experiences and understandings of internationalization, the challenges it presented to participants' theories of learning and teaching, their practical responses to curriculum development, student induction and support and what they regard as worthwhile learning innovation (Errington, 2004).

Perceptions of internationalization

Most of the participants referred to the internationalization agenda in terms of the expansion of postgraduate student numbers. This was unsurprising given the ambitious faculty targets for international student recruitment. The majority of participants viewed the growing diversity of the postgraduate population positively, including a director of postgraduate studies who said that: 'Internationalization is clearly a route that we are going down and it will increase. It can lead to more interesting teaching and learning, an enriching experience.' This recently appointed professor was one of a growing number of international academics in the faculty. Although these appointments appeared to have been driven largely by research imperatives rather than by a broader vision of internationalization in the faculty, some heads noted other benefits for their schools, such as the development of new interdisciplinary postgraduate programmes marketed with an international perspective and an international audience in mind.

While there was general agreement that internationalization is desirable in principle, a minority of staff regarded the growth in international student numbers as an 'unfortunate necessity'. Concerns were voiced about the additional time and effort perceived to be involved in new programme development and in supporting international students, the increases in staff-student ratios, and teaching, supervisory and pastoral responsibilities. These additional demands impacted upon colleagues' research time and hence on their preferred career development. As one head of school said: 'Workload debates have been predominantly about students but highlight tensions between teaching and learning and research. . . . The burden falls heavily on a few key staff, with consequences for their research careers.'

This notion of internationalization as a burden, even in schools with substantial experience in the field, was commonly expressed. Some directors of studies were uncomfortable with the idea of 'marketing' their programmes and were unconvinced about the benefits of having a more diverse student intake. A senior female colleague who managed professional development programmes for health- and education-related professionals commented: 'The idea of having "markets" for us is bizarre. We respond to a training and educational need as specified by [a national body]. Of course we have to attract students, but they have to have the right qualities. It is a reciprocal relationship, not one of consumer and provider.'

Learning and teaching

The majority of participants agreed that the cultural diversity of the student body enriches the teaching and learning experience and 'can be a lot of fun. . . . it can transform the learning environment'. The benefits for learning were largely perceived to result from students sharing experiences and appreciating each other's cultures. However, the growth in diversity was unevenly dispersed across disciplines and some schools had experienced an influx of students from Southeast Asia and China in particular. Several participants alluded to the predominance of Asian students in certain programmes, particularly in business and education studies. There were concerns that students who had selected the university in order to have 'the UK experience' and found themselves in a cohort with few, if any, home students might be disillusioned.

Intercultural discussion and learning may not happen automatically, simply by placing students in intercultural groups. One director of programmes, himself of Asian origin, commented that homogeneous groups tend to 'stick together' to the detriment of the development of 'interpersonal skills and cross-cultural communication [which] is good preparation for the world of work. Normally they overdo their contact with other Chinese students. I constantly warn them against this. [They risk] cultural underachievement.' Another participant considered it the job of the director of studies to work 'to develop cohort identity'. This would undoubtedly prove challenging to those participants who preferred familiar modes of learning and teaching and who referred to the domestic cohort as 'our students', inadvertently designating international students as the cultural 'other'. There were also concerns that home students may not see the benefits of being part of a diverse learning community, and difficulties were anticipated when 'the expectations [of international students] collide with those of small groups of home students'.

Discussions about internationalizing teaching focused largely on programme content rather than pedagogy. Some participants recognized the importance of 'designing postgraduate programmes for an international audience' and there were examples of programmes which drew on tutors' research interests in 'identity, narratives, culture, entrepreneurship and application to pedagogy'. There was, however, a lack of awareness of the cultural nature of teaching and learning practices and cultural pedagogies. There were few examples of programme development based upon pedagogical considerations or recognition of the reciprocal benefits that might be achieved through responsive pedagogies and modes of delivery (De Vita and Case, 2003).

More commonly, Western participatory modes of learning and teaching were perceived to be problematic for Asian students whose learning preferences were rooted in cultures that view teachers as experts (Cortazzi and Jin, 1996; Littlewood and Liu, 1999; Cheng, 2000; Turner and Acker, 2002). International students were thought to be uncomfortable with the reflective, meta-cognitive or self-engagement aspects of learning underpinning Western postgraduate studies (Schon, 1987; Gelter, 2003). A female professor and head of school noted: 'Chinese students may come with a different aesthetic and there can be difficulty about notions of criticality.'

However, two heads of school dismissed the implication that a lack of familiarity with reflective and critical practices has a detrimental impact on learning: 'The implication that Chinese students cannot think critically is nonsense.' 'It is important to approach this with some kind of integrity. I am less inclined now to think this will lower standards.'

Pastoral and academic support

A number of tutors saw the spiritual, moral, and intellectual development of students as part of their role. A programme leader said: 'Taking very good care of students is the most important thing. We offer tutorials every week for each student, very close monitoring of students and their performance, and lots of counselling for students who don't do very well. We must be very caring but at the same time very firm.'

A colleague very experienced in working with international students admitted that he spent extra time and effort on supporting international students: 'A lot of them are the age of my kids. If my kids were in their position, I'd want them to be treated in a way that was different . . . '

Most degree programme directors indicated that they provided additional guidance on a range of academic, pastoral and social matters for international students, but there was a lack of consensus about the degree of independence students were expected to acquire and demonstrate. Participants from education studies noted that international students often require additional support to access necessary information, in assignment writing and research supervision. A participant with long experience as a programme director in the business school felt that the demands made on students, particularly those studying one-year, full-time master's programmes, were too great: 'It's not fair to expect them to cope with culture shock; they need a year to acclimatize.'

A clear articulation of the expectations for learning and teaching was recognized to be vital to induct students into the learning culture. Most schools had developed induction programmes to introduce students to ICT skills and library skills, and to offer explanation and practice opportunities in Western discourse conventions, such as the rules of turn-taking, paired work and group work. This was perceived to require more time and ongoing support than tutors were accustomed to provide for traditional domestic cohorts or for European students.

Discussions about orientation and induction arrangements were largely premised upon promoting understanding of '[our] way of doing things' (Cadman, 2000, p. 480). As one head of school illustrated: 'students who are very good in their own countries may struggle with the expectations here . . . we need to explain the expectations; they need time to assimilate the culture.' A director of postgraduate programmes referred particularly to the need to understand students' differing expectations of assessment and marking procedures: 'North American students can be horrified that they get 60 and are told that this is a good mark here!' One programme director commented on the high level of coaching and tutorial support he considers necessary: 'Feedback is very important and a lot of . . . practice and intensive personal coaching and mentoring.'

Other comments indicated a more inclusive perspective: one tutor commented 'It's difficult to design a truly international course. The challenge is to meet the needs of people with different expectations and backgrounds.' Flexibility in the range of approaches and modes of delivery was considered important. As a head of school commented: 'We need to be really welcoming to different ways of thinking and different approaches.' Other colleagues noted that cultural sensitivity is essential with respect to student expectations, for example regarding participatory teaching (Adams, 2004) and supervisory styles (Harman, 2003) and the demonstration of critical and reflective skills in interactions between tutor and student, or student and student. Comprehensive, long-term support arrangements were considered to be important: 'We've decided not to front-load induction but to spread it out, to coincide with study phases, e.g. plagiarism, assignments, how to interpret feedback . . .'

Ongoing language support was also considered to be important, although some colleagues confused students' language competence with their learning capacity: 'The language problem is cultural/ they need to be able to think for themselves.' A head of school challenged the assumption that proficiency in the language of instruction was related to intellect capacity: 'Not everything is a language problem: teaching is a co-learning experience.' Another participant endorsed this view, stating: 'We need greater understanding of what creates good will. It's all very well to do things to attract students in, but it's what you do when they are here that's important, and that we don't do . . . we don't claim to understand it. We're not listening to students.'

Moving towards inclusive academic experiences and assessment practices

The case study is intended to illuminate some of the challenges to the internationalization process as we move towards more inclusive academic experiences and assessment practices. The concerns highlighted above point to the need for discursive opportunities to address negative conceptions of internationalization, to offer spaces for reflection upon pedagogies and practices, and to support the development of culturally inclusive learning environments (Causey *et al.*, 1999). Winning hearts and minds to the process of internationalization requires innovative approaches to professional engagement (Ho *et al.*, 2001; Ottewill and Macfarlane, 2003; Brew and Peseta, 2004; Gibbs *et al.*, 2000).

The internationalization agenda has created new challenges and opportunities to engage in 'a radical reassessment of the purposes, priorities and processes' of HE (De Vita and Case, 2003, p. 383). This may threaten existing academic identities and support may be necessary to achieve a more holistic approach to internationalization, in which universities become internationally minded communities, not simply institutions with increasingly large numbers of international students (Volet, 1999; Marshall and Martin, 2000; MacKinnon and Manathunga, 2003). Academics inhabit distinct epistemological and social communities (Maassen, 1996) with established narratives, values and practices (Kogan, 2000) that may incline them to resist or subvert change.

Despite the perceived lack of incentives, resources or recognition in HEIs for innovative practice in internationalization (Green, 2003), teacher dispositions have a significant impact on innovation by influencing what is possible, relevant and achievable from the teachers' own governing perspective (Errington, 2004). The teacher plays a key role in mediating knowledge, values and behaviours and intercultural competences. Teachers' beliefs about students influence their instructional approaches, organization of the setting for learning, curriculum content and resources in ways that can impact on students' achievement (Johnson and Inoue, 2003). Professional development for innovation incorporating guided and supported learning, using case studies to promote reflective inquiry, has been found to be successful in providing a rational basis to help teachers identify, articulate and critically evaluate their beliefs (Ottewill and Macfarlane, 2003; Brew and Peseta, 2004).

The majority of participants in our study welcomed the opportunity to take part in reflective discussions about their experiences of internationalization, to revisit their previous assumptions about knowledge and learning (Gibbs and Simpson, 2004) and to share research findings and practices that had proved successful. These opportunities support conceptual change towards a broader vision of internationalization.

Cruickshank (2004) suggests the notion of cultural inclusiveness lies more in the willingness to negotiate learning and teaching strategies, to reflect on values and beliefs and to understand and embrace different ways of knowing, than in the adoption of any specific approach to pedagogy. A number of participants in our study felt that there was little time to reflect upon or adapt pedagogical approaches to take account of diverse student needs. Colleagues with several years of experience of working with relatively large numbers of international students noted that there were rarely structured opportunities to take part in 'intellectually engaging discussion about the issues' which meant that 'positive energy for internationalization is within individuals, not bedded in the school. We've lost our way; we can only skim the surface'.

In reflective discussions about professional experiences, 'the narratives and metaphors by which we structure our lives, the taken-for-granteds, are questioned and challenged' (Bolton, 2005, p. 274). Exploring and optimizing the match between personal and shared views can confront complacency and address concerns in a constructive manner, fostering a more positive cultural climate (Williams, 2005). Conceptual change can lead to change in practices, which are detected by students as qualitative improvements in their learning experiences (Ho *et al.*, 2001).

The internationalization of the curriculum and the values it incorporates demand openness and cosmopolitanism (Rizvi, 2000, p. 8). A shift in focus from problematizing the international student to reviewing teaching methods, content and processes can provide a more inclusive learning environment for other students who may not understand the implicit rules and norms of the HEI, for example mature students who have not engaged in formal education for some years, or non-traditional learners from diverse domestic cohorts (Leonard and Morley, 2003).

Mackinnon and Manathunga (2003) note that teaching and learning in Anglophone universities frequently privileges the dominant cultural literacy. Curriculum, teaching and assessment reviews can ensure that diverse cultural and community literacies are represented and enable students to explore their personal interests and cultural perspectives in meaningful learning engagement (Gregory and Williams, 2000, cited in Mackinnon and Manathunga, 2003, p. 131).

Assessment that generates personal engagement is stimulated by clearly and unambiguously stated assessment goals and explicit expectations that make clear, for example, the need to critically engage with current research literature, to read beyond the set course reading list, or to explore international perspectives. Inevitably in discussions about assessment, Western concepts of authorship and intellectual property are raised. Literacy practices regarded as plagiarism in the West have been explored through the understandings of students from diverse cultures (Robinson and Kuin, 1999; Sowden, 2005) and the assumed stability and universality of 'plagiarism' as a construct is contested. These issues are discussed further in Chapter 6 in which we highlight the importance of expanded student induction and support mechanisms to take account of the challenging, complex and co-constructed nature of academic literacy, and to provide adequate opportunities for students to engage with a range of materials and events in a supported environment (Gourlay, 2006).

Internationalization can involve different levels of engagement, from the practical/technical early levels of engagement to 'relational participation', a more consciously inclusive stance (McTaggart, 2003, p. 7). Bond (2003) influenced by Mestenhauser (1998) and Banks (1999), proposed a three-stage approach with a continuum from 'Add-on' (curriculum that simply adds new international content) to 'Infusion' (integrating more diverse content into the core fabric of the course) to 'Transformational' changes in academics' pedagogy and the learning support environment and students' thinking, that align to Bartell's (2003) theory of transformational internationalization.

Engaging in dialogue about pedagogical issues, personal and shared theories of learning may help participants to identify and articulate their tacit understandings and beliefs, their 'personal practical knowledge' (Bolton, 2005; Errington, 2004), and to address negative conceptions that may impact on the quality of the student experience (Johnson and Inoue, 2003), leading to transformational engagement. Interdisciplinary and inter-institutional networks and communities for practice sharing and research might focus on:

- researching cultures and scholarship of learning and teaching
- disseminating research findings
- collaborative development activities (for academic, research and support staff) to enhance intercultural knowledge, competencies and attitudes necessary for successful internationalization
- evaluating and benchmarking existing institutional practices
- coordinated development activities for postgraduate researchers in the region
- collaborative bid writing for research and development in the above fields
- researching ways to improve the experience of international students/curriculum and pedagogical issues/tutoring and supervising international students
- sharing understandings and teaching innovations in the area of internationalization
- developing a methodology for internationalizing modules and programmes

The final 'destination' may be less important than the process accompanying its development, but there can be little doubt that providing opportunities for colleagues and students to participate in genuine discussion and involvement in determining the scope, penetration and content of an 'internationalization' agenda is a necessary prerequisite for an inclusive culture (Figure 5.2), given the personal and psychological adjustments required to achieve a shift from ethnocentric to ethnorelative orientations in academic lives (Bennett, 1993).

Figure 5.2: Conceptions of internationalization

Conceptions of internationalization		
Problematizing international students Lack of incentive or intrinsic motivation Heavy workload ? → Ethnocentric views: They come for the British experience, don't they? Enculturation of students into 'our way of doing things' Sacrificing research career	Reflective practice Intrinsic motivation Intercultural elements integral to curriculum Learner-centred teaching approaches → Ethnorelative views, mediating knowledge, values and behaviours (intercultural competencis) Reciprocal learning and collaboration in the renegotiation of curriculum, teaching and learning practices, and learning support Discourse communities	Inclusive culture

Chapter 6

Supporting the learning process

This chapter extends the previous discussion about the contribution of social and cultural learning by focusing on the importance of student support in the diverse HE environment. It evaluates the role of both pastoral and academic support in the learning process. The chapter explores the role of study skills development for students and the pivotal importance of academic support to help students progress through learning transitions. The chapter addresses the support required at key points in the student career in the university: pre-departure; arrival and induction; approaching first assessments; projects and dissertations; managing underachievement; preparation for completion; and post-graduation.

Introduction

The increase in the number of international students, along with changes in the ethnic mix of students living in Anglophone countries, has presented challenges for HE. In New Zealand the influx of Asian students led to government initiatives such as the Code of Practice for the Pastoral Care of International Students and an export education levy, introduced in order to ensure that institutions were realistic in their plans for growth in student numbers and attended to factors that contribute to a positive experience for students. The New Zealand Ministry of Education has funded a range of research trials and evaluations of initiatives designed to promote positive student interactions, e.g. through peer-pairing and cooperative learning, and provided workshops for HEIs to facilitate the management of international students' and first nations student' support needs in areas such as academic literacy, classroom management, and teaching and learning styles (Ministry of Education, 2002b).

In the US the American Council on Education has a similar remit to coordinate and disseminate research findings on Global Learning for All, focusing not only on comprehensive internationalization issues but also on the quality of the student experience for minority groups in HE (American Council on Education, 2007).

In the UK, institutions are faced with the dilemma of devising cost-effective methods of delivery (Bamford *et al.*, 2002) while maintaining a world-class reputation and high-quality student experience (Prime Minister's Initiative, PMI 2, April 2006). PMI2 served as a timely reminder that research and strategic developments around internationalization have for too long been dominated by a focus on recruitment rather than ensuring the value of the product (Walker, 1999) and have resulted in parallel rather than integrated thinking about international and domestic minority cohorts.

A focus on models of learning, and student expectations and understandings of the HE learning process, can inform the provision of academic and pastoral support to help students to progress smoothly through learning transitions. While the need to provide a quality experience and support the learning of international students may be our primary aim, there are advantages for all students in the modifications to the learning environment and climate of support.

Models of learning

A range of factors influence students' learning in HE (Newton and Newton, 1997). Students engaged in the same task can produce multiple outcomes, as individuals are influenced in different ways by the learning context, the tutor, their individual perceptions of the task and their preferred approaches to learning (Gibbs, 1995, cited in Newton and Newton, 1997). The extent to which individuals recall and connect facts and strategies learned earlier to the current task, hypothesize and experiment with relationships, take risks, review progress, collect new information, seek help, and seek personal meaning in the task, will impact on emerging understandings.

If students are to be assured a positive learning experience then it is important that their understanding about learning coincides with what is considered as successful learning in the HEI. Säljö (1979) identified student conceptions of learning that included memorizing, acquiring facts, increasing knowledge and developing understanding. Tutors also have individual conceptions of learning and of their roles in relation to imparting information, transferring knowledge, facilitating understanding and nurturing deep approaches to learning (Newton and Newton, 1997; Marton and Säljö, 1976).

The Higher Education Funding Council (HEFC) and the Higher Education Academy (HEA) have commissioned a range of studies that improve our understanding of teacher and learner perspectives and conceptions of learning. Figure 6.1 illustrates a range of ways in which learning activities may be planned in response to individual and collective needs, motives, learning styles and prior experience; to plan the physical context, resources and services required; to emphasize the social context of learning, and engagement in communities of practice; to design the curricular content and pedagogical approach to the learning activity and intended learning outcomes (HEFC, 2006).

Figure 6.1: Perspectives on learning. Adapted from Higher Education Funding Council (2006), p.15. 'Innovative practice with e-learning'

Perspective	The learner
The associative perspective	Knowledge acquired and associations built between concepts Progressively complex actions developed from component skills
The constructivist perspective (individual focus)	New ideas constructed by building and testing hypotheses
The constructivist perspective (social focus)	Understanding achieved through dialogue and active construction of new ideas
The situated perspective	Individual and collective identity developed through participation in communities and practices

The relationships between conceptions of learning outcomes (such as cognitive development, academic and professional identity and personal identity and self-knowledge) and the ways in which learning is mediated by curricula, assessment, people and the social context of study illustrate a clear association between students' conceptions of learning and their approaches to studying (the 'What is Learned at University: The Social and Organisational Mediation of University Learning' (SOMUL) project 2004–2007. www.open.ac.uk/cheri/SOMULsummary.htm).

Connections are suggested, for example, between reconstructive conceptions of learning and deep approaches to study and, in contrast, links between reproductive conceptions of learning and surface approaches to studying. This suggests that students have distinct learning patterns or learning styles (Vermunt, 2005), although the

SOMUL data suggests that personal change and development are more strongly associated with students' varied experiences while they are at university than with the learning patterns that they acquired earlier (Richardson and Edmunds, 2007), in line with constructionist and situated perspectives, in which students' identity develops through participating in discourse communities and practices.

These findings complement earlier research on successful learning. In a learner-centred curriculum well-designed activities and experiences can help students to gain autonomy, develop self-regulatory skills, and improve their ability to set task goals, to plan strategies for achieving these goals efficiently, and to monitor and evaluate their own progress towards these goals (Butler, 1998; Moseley *et al.*, 2004). Self-knowledge is central to successful learning (Moon, 2003) and can be developed through systematic support and individual effort to enable individuals to select and attain learning challenges and goals that match their interests, abilities, values and personal motivations (Pascarella and Terenzini, 2005, cited in Richardson and Edmunds, 2007).

The learning support environment

McTaggart (2003, p. 3) suggests that an inclusive approach to supporting successful learning will embrace pedagogy, curriculum and the learning support environment. What is refreshing about this approach to policy development and quality assurance is that it encourages explicit reflection about change, offering principles and/or practical examples tried elsewhere as a 'resource rather than a series of prescriptions'.

Consideration of issues such as how learning is organized, where it takes place, who the learner is learning with, and what support they may require will have practical and pedagogical implications for tutors. Understanding of the complex range of influences on the student experience, such as their motivations and reasons for studying, their expectations of the study programme, and awareness of what else is happening in their lives while studying, e.g. the need or desire to do paid work, and the extent and nature of their other commitments and living arrangements, etc., is important to the planning and design of the overall climate of support (Turner, 2006b; Devos, 2003).

Huczynski and Buchanan (2001) describe a three-stage model of the socialization process for newly arrived students comprising pre-arrival, encounter and metamorphosis. We used data from a small-scale research project investigating the experience of 42 international postgraduate students who took part in focus groups at our own institution to illuminate the support required at each of the first two stages (pre-arrival; on encounter). Our survey of student conceptions took place during two-year teaching fellowships when we explored both staff and student perceptions of internationalization. Specifically we were able to tap students' perceptions of the institution as an international university, and to investigate student needs and concerns at the three stages of the socialization process (Huczynski and Buchanan, 2001). This leads to consideration of the conditions necessary to enable students to achieve transformational change (metamorphosis).

Pre-arrival

The quality of support impacts upon the student experience long before the individual arrives at the host institution. Focus group data revealed a range of reasons why students had selected the university as their first choice for study. Their decisions were influenced by their perceptions of administrative factors such as prompt replies to applications and enquiries, support with accommodation arrangements and childcare, good online and face-to-face support from administrative and academic staff, and early identification of key people such as their personal tutor and supervisor. Many of the factors identified related to the frequency, timeliness and quality of personal interactions.

Encounter: on arrival

The orientation and induction programme is an important element of most universities' initial welcome to students on arrival. The availability of practical support on arrival, to help for example with various registration procedures, e.g. for study programmes, travel cards, at the bank and with a doctor, is important as many students encounter difficulties in understanding registration systems, compounded by problems in understanding the English that is spoken to them and in making themselves understood.

Effective induction is unlikely to be achieved in the first few weeks of the study period and will ideally continue to provide support for several months after arrival. Social anxiety in intercultural interactions in newly arrived students is common (Mak *et al.*, 1999). Students may be unfamiliar with the social values and rules governing interpersonal relationships in the host environment and this may hinder their participation in educational and social interactions. Early contact with ethnic or faith-based societies and communities, introductions to host families and peer-pairing or 'buddy' systems were welcomed. The activities on offer during the orientation week and the emphasis on alcohol-related social activities were a source of concern for many international students and inhibited contact with home students.

Newly arrived students may be overwhelmed in the early weeks by the unfamiliarity of the physical and sociocultural environment and may need time to orient themselves to their surroundings before feeling ready to work towards setting communication goals or to interpret the values, norms and learning expectations of the host institution and their specific programme of study (Zepke and Leach, 2005). Getting the timing right for competency training is crucial.

While skills training for the development of sociocultural competency does not guarantee students educational success, being socially confident and achieving a sense of identity in the host country can significantly enhance interpersonal communication and inclusion in social networks, contributing to individual well-being. Learning to speak up or presenting one's ideas or opinions to a group are key sociocultural competencies needed in social and study- or work-related situations. Coaching and opportunities to practise competencies in real social situations was considered to be useful, e.g. the social skills required for job interviews; to deal with noisy neighbours; to negotiate an arrangement for working with a tutor that meets their individual needs; or to negotiate an extension to the due date of an academic assignment (Mak *et al.*, 1999).

Simply explaining the conventions for study to students or focusing on language support and study skills strategies (Cadman, 2000; Zepke and Leach, 2005) is not adequate to facilitate change. Modelling of skills and opportunities to practise unfamiliar skills in a supportive environment can be more helpful (Cadman, 2000), although implicit in these approaches is a remediation of students' existing language and cultural norms as barriers to successful integration. Student outcomes are influenced by the ways in which they perceive that their cultural attributes are valued and the differences between them are bridged (Zepke and Leach, 2005; Jones, 2005). An assimilationist approach that fails to recognize the identities and experiences of students may have a detrimental affect on their self-concept (Cadman, 2000; Liddicoat, 2004).

Some students may require assistance to develop self-understanding in supportive environments that provide substantive formative feedback and encourage development of autonomy and self-reflection (Moon, 2003). Others may find tools and frameworks, such as the thinking skills frameworks discussed in the previous chapter, helpful for self-monitoring and management of learning and to deepen meta-cognitive awareness at an individual, group and community level (Moseley *et al.*, 2004). Sternberg (2003) argues that motivation is the driving force that enables successful learners to achieve a synthesis of wisdom, intelligence and creativity in their learning. Renzulli and Reis (1986) also regard high intelligence and creativity as vital, but describe task commitment as the third essential component of successful learning. However well motivated and committed students are, student success will be dependent upon the match between their perceived criteria for success and the actual criteria in the institution.

Induction

Induction programmes can play an important role in addressing a mismatch between student and institutional understandings and learning objectives. However, induction programmes that require students to attend extra 'study skills' sessions in their busy schedule place additional pressures on individuals and denote 'otherness', and imply that acculturation or remediation of deficits in the student is necessary. Culturally sensitive teaching, on the other hand, does not involve special treatment or assessment of international students. Varied and flexible teaching methods and tasks can be introduced to improve understanding about diverse educational and cultural traditions and to challenge all students to think in more complex ways about their identities and histories (Johnson and Inoue, 2003).

Inclusive approaches drawing on constructivist perspectives acknowledge diverse students' world-views with 'a two-way flow of ideas and values between communities' (Barnett, 1994, as cited in Kelly, 1999, p. 20) in and out of formal educational settings, and in the 'hidden curriculum' (Snyder, 1971). This assists cultural understanding and the social mediation of learning (Pascarella and Terenzini, 2005, cited in Richardson and Edmunds, 2007).

Provision of discursive opportunities for students to explore their experiences and beliefs about learning and make learning expectations explicit can help to build confidence and assist student adjustment (Chanock, 2004). Erlenawati (2005) highlighted the ways in which both the cultural conventions and the social situation in which language interaction is embedded shape student experiences. Bretag *et al.* (2002) found a barrier to learning was created when students had incomplete understanding of lecturers' spoken English, and had difficulty interpreting colloquial language. These concerns may be addressed by engaging students in informal discourses and practical or experiential opportunities for engagement with the institutional culture, language, knowledge frameworks and theoretical understandings embedded in teaching programmes (Padilla *et al.*, 1997, cited in Zepke and Leach, 2005).

Integrating intercultural and social learning skills

Increasingly programme designers are integrating intercultural skills and competencies as accredited elements of degree programmes. Much of the literature focuses on the Asian/Western dichotomy and the knowledge tradition of Chinese students and its impact on their adjustment to Anglophone teaching and learning dynamics, particularly in undergraduate business programmes (Cortazzi and Jin, 2001). Turner's (2006) research with Chinese learners in postgraduate study in the UK, reported in Chapter 3, indicated that in demanding one-year courses students have little time to do more than grapple with and conform to UK academic conventions and learning standards. They acquire new skills and knowledge, but their attitudes to learning are relatively unaffected by their experience of study in the UK. While generally successful in their degrees, much of what they experience in learning may be relatively superficial rather than transformational (Turner, 2006).

Academic success is intrinsic to students' general sense of well-being and confidence. In order to succeed in UK postgraduate contexts, students are required to understand the discursive nature of learning, to acquire the habit to reflect on their own experience and, perhaps most challenging, to offer a critical perspective on diverse theories, knowledges and literatures. Critical evaluation skills are assessed as an essential element of graduate studies to achieve deep understanding of the subject of study, rather than 'surface' approaches focusing on instrumental aspects of task and memorization.

Interpreting assessment criteria and feedback is not always straightforward. One student wondered what a tutor meant when he was told that he had submitted 'a solid piece of work' when, from his own perception, a mark of 60 per cent was a great disappointment, compared with the sort of marks he had achieved in his home university. Students may need personal, social and emotional support, as well as learning support, to accommodate to the norms underpinning teaching, learning and assessment and succeed academically.

Students' early encounters with teaching methods based on social learning theory (Bandura, 1977) frequently involve multicultural group work, 'buddy' or mentoring systems. Common requirements for interactive learning which require, for example, assessment of oral presentations can create anxiety. Other worries frequently mentioned by students include meeting and greeting new people, knowing where to go for assistance, guidance and advice, time management and understanding academic writing and citation/referencing conventions.

Study methods incorporating peer learning and, increasingly, interactions with technology, can support the development of interdependent, collaborative learning (Butler, 1998; Jones and Merritt, 1999; Livingstone *et al.*, 2004). Face-to-face contact between tutors, learners and peers can be supported by virtual learning environments (VLE) and well-managed online discussion. The online component of programmes can help to maximize learning, enabling students to access lecture notes, key papers, case studies, problem-based learning scenarios and other resources in their own time, at their own pace and in their chosen work environment.

Individual engagement with online learning resources serves as the basis for collaborative online discussion, either in real time or through asynchronous discussion boards. To facilitate e-learning, it is important that the tutor sets clear guidelines for discussion fora, monitors their use, and interjects with timely questions and feedback to individuals and the forum to stimulate the discussion and deepen learning (HEFCE, 2004).

There are benefits to students from interactions with peers from other countries and different backgrounds, although some students chose to come to England to experience an English system. When fellow students are thought to be interested in and encourage participants to talk about their own culture this influences their approach to course work and choice of research topics. However, this may not always be the case. Students may be disappointed that many of the British students on their course do not appear to be interested in where they came from or their culture: 'British people hard to socialize with'.

This suggests that there is a need to change the culture of the institution to develop a more reciprocal approach to understanding, teaching and supporting international students. Ward's (2001) research suggests that international students expect and desire contact with domestic peers, and that positive social, psychological and academic benefits arise from these contacts; however, the amount of interaction between international and domestic students may be low and the presence of international students alone is not sufficient to foster intercultural friendships.

On a more positive note the multicultural experience in modules and degree programmes can be enhanced when students are taught by staff who themselves have international experience, or through having tutors who are non-British, and through the introduction to international case studies, theories and policies in the curriculum. This encourages engagement with broader learning theories through reflection and discussion and consideration of the implications and relevance for their own contexts.

In Europe many HEIs are integrating mandatory courses on international and intercultural issues into their programmes in order to develop students' broader perspectives, intercultural competency, critical thinking and comparative thinking (Yershova *et al.*, 2000). The diversity-sensitive curriculum (Chang and Astin, 1997) has been reported to have positive effects on students' academic achievement and personal development, irrespective of their race and culture, helping to bridge differences, both on campus and in society. Students from a business school, for example, felt that the curriculum could be more international if more varied case studies were introduced and seminar themes rather than focusing on on British or European perspectives, representing a wider range of cultural perspectives.

Social and pastoral support

Opportunities to meet English families, to take part in home stay arrangements and join family and community events are welcomed by many international students. If students have chosen their university because they want to have 'the British experience' then immersion in the language, the traditions and local environment will be important aspects of the learning experience. Other students who have had different motivations for selecting the university (its research culture, or its international perspective) may seek other forms of social support. Commonly students gravitate towards their own ethnic group in student societies, in living arrangements, and in group-learning tasks for social support.

When students become isolated or experience problems of adjustment, universities have structured welfare services to provide academic and personal counselling and practical and pastoral support. However, the existence of a comprehensive range of services does not necessarily lead to uptake by the students most in need of support. In a study for the Ministry of Education in New Zealand, Ward (2003) found that over half of her respondents evaluated institutional services and facilities as necessary and valuable. Yet despite these positive evaluations, students appeared to be relatively uninformed about the actual availability of services. These findings suggest the need for comprehensive strategies to publicize relevant information to international students about available support and how to access it.

Some institutions are developing integrated international advisory services and facilities for language support, health and welfare services, counselling, accommodation services, vocational/careers guidance, computing services and learning support that is responsive to the increasing diversity of student needs, offering informal, drop-in support. The key role of the international student adviser has emerged with a range of interpretations and functions in different institutions, but generally the focus is very much on practical support, particularly pre- and on-arrival. This 'one-stop shop' approach was favoured by students from our own institution.

Language support

Students from non-English-speaking countries, students from regions where English is used as a second or official language, but also students for whom English is the language of instruction in their home countries, have found to their dismay that understanding English as spoken in the host community, and in different ways within the host university, can represent a significant challenge. Over 70 per cent of Bamford *et al.*'s (2002) East Asian respondents stated that they regarded improving their English proficiency as a means to improve their career prospects. Some of Bamford *et al.*'s (2002) interviewees mentioned that they had found it necessary to take part-time work in order to support themselves and pay their fees, but this was a useful way to gain insights into the English way of life and to practise English language skills.

Many students comment that teachers and domestic students simply speak too fast. Students who are not fluent may miss the subtlety of a particular discussion point, feel embarrassed that their English is not adequate to contribute to the discussion, which leads to frustration and reduced participation. Opportunities for informal conversation can be helpful, and peer-pairing or buddying systems can facilitate this. Academic assignment writing may also present significant challenges, disadvantaging students for whom English is a second or third language (Gil and Katsara, 1999).

Learning support

Access to appropriate learning support can help to ensure that students understand Western cultural pedagogy and the expectations for participation in class and assignment completion. We have discussed in earlier chapters how cultural differences between Chinese students and Western students influence their experience of the British higher education system. For example the Confucian influence on classroom behaviour may be interpreted to lead students to follow, without question, the decisions of the teacher (Martinsons and Martinsons, 1996); to attempt to acquire 'a vast store of knowledge through rote memorisation' (Chan, 1999: p. 298); and to honour teachers through memorizing and reproducing their words, or movements and images in the Arts. This can cause confusion and anxiety when students are faced with Western conventions about plagiarism. Practice assignments and formative feedback can make the expectations for 'finding one's own voice' clear and provide opportunities to paraphrase, reflect and critique the author's views.

Discussion, reflection and meta-cognition or self-engagement aspects of thinking feature strongly in Western postgraduate programmes. Possession of higher-order skills is considered necessary to interpret information, to plan effectively, to work collaboratively and to make informed decisions. Reflection is a key element of the action research process (Gelter, 2003), and a key factor in Kolb's (1984) theory of experiential learning.

Gelter (2003) suggests that reflection is a learned process of historically recent origin, arising in cultures based on democracy and may be problematic for students from cultures where subordination of personal aspirations for the collective good are the norm. There may be cultural obstacles to the implementation of reflective practices in interactions between men and women or superior and subordinate within research groups or networks. Developing reflective behaviour may require dedicated time, effort and support (Gelter, 2003) and may be enhanced through student observation of another person successfully modelling the behaviour (Adams, 2000). Caruana (2004) notes the irony that internationalization increases awareness and recognition of the idea that knowledge is culture-bound.

Adams' research with a group of international postgraduate research students investigated whether self-efficacy was enhanced more by observing an 'expert' model (a university lecturer) or a 'non-expert' peer model (a more experienced student). In this study, observation of peer presenters significantly enhanced the confidence and efficacy of international students, compared with students who observed expert models (Adams, 2000, p. 126). Adams suggests that peer models can be a valuable resource for teaching academic seminar presentation skills and other communicative tasks, such as proposal and thesis writing. Prompt feedback from peers and tutors on assignments can also reduce performance anxiety.

Key relationships

Adrian-Taylor *et al.* (2007) emphasize that for graduate students, the relationship with their supervisor is particularly important to overall satisfaction and success. The supervisor's role is interpreted to encompass clarifying and negotiating expectations and demonstrating interest in students' professional development. The quality of the supervisor-supervisee relationship has been linked to stress reduction and student well-being (Mallinckrodt and Leong, 1992, p. 76, cited in Adrian-Taylor *et al.*, 2007).

In addition to the relationship with a key person, a sense of belonging within the academic community is important to student well-being and success. The emergence of the Community of Practice (CoP), grounded in theories of learning as social participation (Wenger, 1998; Bandura, 1977), allows more subtle types of knowledge-sharing through common activities, practices, resources and information (Clark and Brennan, 1991). Narration (storytelling) may be used to represent and share existing knowledge and generate knowledge (Brown and Duguid, 1991). Wenger (1998) proposed a view of the organization as a constellation of interrelated CoPs: membership of CoPs may overlap with each other within and across organizations, facilitating transfer of knowledge and learning through social links.

Williams (2005) also describes the university as a cultural community made up of sub-cultures, each with their own discourse and shared understandings. Social and cultural influences, and earlier exposure to differing educational provisions and technologies, will have a significant impact on the development of meaning and understandings (Williams, 2005). Novice members of the CoP will require induction into the discourses and enhanced opportunities to practise skills and consolidate learning. The challenge for the host community is to develop ways in which international student identities are affirmed, their cultural attributes are valued, and cultural differences are bridged (Zepke and Leach, 2005; Thomas, 2002).

For postgraduate students the needs may be particularly acute, given the cultural, social and academic adjustments required in order to manage the demands of intense, full-time programmes which, in the

UK, are frequently of only one year's duration. Support is important at key points in the student career, from pre-departure to post-graduation.

Inclusive programme development

Separate study skills programmes reflect a transmission approach to teaching and a remedial model. Where skills are taught in isolation from the contexts for their use, learning transfer may be poor (Biggs, 1999, as cited in Warren, 2005). However, the provision of a learning community for social and academic support, offering opportunities for discussion of issues or concerns and guided reflection, with a regular 'drop-in' arrangement supplemented by a VLE and discussion forum, may have some merit.

A postgraduate student community has developed at our own institution in response to student perceptions of their support needs and desire for regular face-to-face contact with key tutors and with each other. Beginning with an induction conference and a range of social activities early in the academic year, students are encouraged to get to know each other across disciplines and ethnicities. Some specific discussion and practical sessions are offered throughout the academic year, such as:

- ICT skills audit and training, e.g. to ensure that students have the skills to conducting a literature review online, use electronic journals, etc., and to ensure that students are not disadvantaged in terms of access to blended learning opportunities
- Setting up your study group
- Living as a student, sharing accommodation and communication issues
- Approaching the first assignment
- Independent study, learning styles and approaches
- Finding and using academic information
- Preparing and submitting group assignments
- Understanding and using feedback
- Preparing and delivering oral presentations
- Getting started on research projects and portfolio work
- Managing the relationship with your supervisor
- Engaging with local community groups and voluntary sector organizations
- What to do if your marks are not what you expected: preparing for resits and resubmissions
- Managing the final stages of project and dissertation work

In addition, students can 'drop-in' to either face-to-face or online discussions that unpack the expectations for study at the university, address issues and concerns, and provide a forum for the sharing of ideas.

In an ideal learning environment, all the expectations about learning and teaching would be embedded in programme content and delivery and explicitly negotiated with students. In an imperfect environment where conflicting pressures between teaching and research continue to vex overburdened academics, and staff skills and curriculum audits with respect to internationalization are ongoing, it seems sensible to offer students access to a community for conversation, to enhance language and reflective skills, discussion about experiences, and timely access to skills audit and enhancement as needs arise. Informal communication between teachers and students can help to reframe traditional teacher-student hierarchical relationships and move the community towards increased reciprocity and interculturality (Bretag, 2006).

Metamorphosis: an inclusive culture or climate on campus

Internationalization is an ongoing process of institutional improvement incorporating ethos, activities, content and graduate attributes (Caruana and Hanstock, 2005). This will involve curriculum modifications to make the content and modes of delivery more meaningful and relevant for students from different cultures, and to prepare students from home and other cultures to live, learn or work in international settings (McTaggart, 2003). By explicitly focusing on inclusive teaching and learning strategies for all, students' 'international' streams or colonial legacies can be eradicated. Instead of providing information, the teacher's role is to create and facilitate challenging collaborative learning spaces (Caruana, 2004). This requires a cultural shift in the institution and supportive professional development opportunities so that the international dimension is a mainstreamed, integral part of the design and assessment of learning activities and experiences for domestic and international students, so-called Internationalization at Home.

Shifting away from a limited conceptualization of internationalization as recruitment of international students, to a wider ranging and more inclusive strategy that appreciates all learning perspectives, is vital to transformational internationalization. Student mobility offers new experiences, but new understandings will only emerge from intercultural responsivity (Caruana, 2004).

Chapter 7

Managing the process: strategic and management issues

Introduction: internationalization and the management imperative

This chapter aims to explore some of the key practical institutional issues that have emerged within earlier chapters. As we have discussed, the impacts of internationalization are wide-ranging and affect institutional strategy, operations and systems infrastructure. As we have also suggested, its workings are contradictory and at times may appear incoherent. To some extent, therefore, internationalization acts as an institutional catalyst for change, prompting the need for management responses across a range of core organizational functions (Walters and Adams, 2001). Yet the degree to which – as a dynamic and emergent organizational force – internationalization is susceptible to planned, directive management approaches is also open to debate (Edwards and Usher, 1997; Taylor, 2004). Nonetheless, in spite of the unpredictable influence of global forces and the uncertainties posed by the management of internationalization at organizational level, the imperative for effective institutional management in internationalizing environments seems emphatic because: 'It is usually at the individual, institutional level that the real process of internationalization is taking place' (Knight, 2004, pp. 6–7).

As a way of beginning to penetrate the broad range and scope of the management challenges which boundary internationalization, we have focused on the twin themes of Managing Diversity (Staff, Programmes and Students), and Managing the Process of Internationalization, summarized at Figure 7.1. Inevitably these two themes cannot provide an exhaustive list under which to marshal operational priorities for management action in responding to internationalization. They do, however, reflect the key strategic themes that emerge most powerfully from the practice-based literature and coalesce to suggest a broad action framework for management within internationalizing institutions in a range of contexts.

Figure 7.1: Strategic themes in the management of internationalization

Programme diversity	Student diversity	Staff diversity
• Multi-channel/multi-site delivery, including international partnerships and collaborative arrangements • International massification • International delivery • Uneven demand distribution	• Provision and mix of support • Internationalization at Home • Intercultural diversity management • Extended student careers	• Academic/professional development • International career management and planning • Local vs. international pedagogies

Organizational context
- Local/national setting
- Institutional focus
- Management and policy systems and infrastructure
- International orientation/aspirations

The process of internationalization
- Managing international resources
- The role of the international office
- Values management
- Balancing centralization and decentralization
- Embedding internationalization

Managing international diversity

Staff

As we have indicated in earlier chapters, one of the key early indicators of incipient internationalization within HE across a range of contexts has been the increased mobility of academic staff. It is no surprise therefore that the management of international staff mobility presents a key challenge within internationalizing institutions, particularly in countries like the UK and Australia which are witnessing continuing and growing academic immigration. In recent years it has become common for institutions to respond to the wider forces of educational globalization and increased staff mobility by putting into place recruitment systems that are capable of extending staff searches overseas. In response to this alongside other changes in academic work patterns many institutional systems have developed into fully flexible organizations – following patterns familiar in international corporate organizations – which have expanded the organization's periphery and utilize a range of short- and fixed-term contracts for non-local academic workers (Marginson, 2000). The broader impact of such changes has been a matter of debate within the HE management literature (Lewis and Altbach, 1996; Clark, 1997; Dearlove, 1998; Szekeres, 2006). In respect of internationalization, however, such approaches have tended to function relatively simply by bringing in young cross-border academic workers in particular into contract research or training grades within HEIs.

Within this context, the implications of international mobility for more established local tenured staff are also significant and may not yet be fully recognized within university employment systems, beyond the long-established international character of elite research careers. Certainly the implications of international mobility for academic identity, careers and professional development seem significant (Bekhradnia and Sastry, 2005). The management of increasing diversity of employment patterns and a growing international workforce presents a clear priority within internationalizing institutions, therefore. Particularly in the context of declining academic salaries and status, efforts aimed at stabilizing staff turnover introduce increasing complexity into HR management systems. In earlier chapters we have discussed the teaching and learning implications identified in the practice literature of diverse cohorts taught largely by teachers with little international experience. In addition to basic recruitment and retention issues, therefore, the workforce management challenge within internationalizing environments is to establish academic career management systems to proactively support intercultural development. This can be achieved through systems of international postings, sabbaticals and exchanges which aim to achieve professional development for teachers as much as for researchers. Accompanying the development of such systems is a range of complex implications for institutions, academic workers and also for their dependants and family members. In the past, where such overseas postings have been research-led, many HEIs have established passive response systems to facilitate short-term overseas activities. The stimuli for such activities, however, have often originated with academics rather than with institutions and supported by external research funding rather than from direct institutional resources. The degree to which international exchanges for professional teaching development have been institutionally recognized and supported appears far less. The staffing implications inherent in the management of larger-scale, longer-term transnational education projects and overseas branch campuses are also significant, as we will discuss below, forcing management and policy considerations of the status of staff employed in such projects, as well as prompting the need to provide support for their welfare while in post overseas. In general, a simple reliance upon short-term contracted staff for international activities, while offering an apparently expedient management response to the uncertainties of internationalization, may risk the loss of valuable intercultural learning that could be harnessed more widely within institutions. It may also fail to support more established staff – outside research elites – who might benefit considerably from international rotation within their career development. Historically, the degree to which institutions have actively engaged with academic staff in international career planning seems relatively low – in spite of the attractiveness to institutions of international experience in recruitment terms. Internationalization, then, implies increasing complexity and diversity in core as well as peripheral staffing and the need for institutions proactively to organize the contribution of international experience to career development for their current and future staffing. The implications for HR policies, staffing continuity and professional development provision are clear. Additional staff management impacts also arise out of institutional language, curriculum and pedagogical policy development in the face of international strategic aspirations.

Students

Linking to the management of staff, the management of student diversity is a key discussion within institutional case studies and the practice-based literature. A range of issues come to the fore, primarily focusing on the challenges inherent in the management of students' expectations against their experiences. Particularly where international students pay premium fees, they are likely to bring high expectations to their study experiences. Students are also increasingly identifying themselves as 'customers' of HE services which encourages them to articulate any concerns they may have about quality of service delivery. Given the contribution of relationship and alumni marketing in the international context, the future recruitment impacts of reports from unsatisfied returnees are potentially significant. The consequent emphasis on the management of institutional student services is significant. Student diversity implies a concomitant diversity of expectations about appropriate levels and ranges of service availability and their quality, bringing increasing complexity to the design and organization of university service systems. Student diversity also brings different expectations about basic educational processes and outcomes, as we have discussed in preceding chapters. In general, the implication for institutions is on highly proactive service provision, anticipating and normalizing diversity of demand. Historically, relatively passive support systems have evolved to meet the demands and expectations of local students, who, as cultural insiders, were equipped with sufficient local knowledge to enable them to access available services. Institutional responsibility for students in internationalizing environments, however, requires a developed sense of 'active hosting' from service providers if new arrivals are to be effectively initiated into the institutional community. This results in a complex mix of service provision, stretching the notion of the student career through a wide range of service stages from pre-entry to alumni, highlighted at Figure 7.2.

Within this context of the management of international student diversity, it is also important to recognize that many cross-border students are seeking an international experience alongside an academic one during their studies. These expectations require active decision making to determine the boundaries around institutional responsibility for students' personal lives. Evidence suggests that many cross-border students take a broad view of institutional responsibility, including support in aspects of their personal and domestic lives which HEIs may not have taken fully into account and which extend beyond the provision of therapeutic or remedial student welfare services (Turner,

Figure 7.2: Support Service Mix for across the student career

Pre-entry:
Service emphasis: *Information management*
Including:
Institutional marketing
Recruitment information
Financial information
League tables and quality measures
Immigration and visa information
Student life information
Recruitment agent management

Admissions:
Service emphasis: *Admissions management*
Including:
Admissions information
Advice and support with application process
Initial academic induction (introducing the student experience)
Family liaison

Pre-departure:
Service emphasis: *Personal welfare support*
Including:
Pre-departure briefings, to host institution and host country
Travel support
General pre-departure information
Active visa application support

Arrival:
Service emphasis: *Personal welfare support/integrated administrative services*
Including:
Accommodation
Finance
Welfare/student support
Orientation: institutional locality
General introduction to department and programme of study
Language and study support

Induction:
Service emphasis: *Information provision and problem solving*
Including:
Academic induction including local academic conventions
Personal/academic tutoring
Personal and academic Network development support
Student services (language support, information resources, etc.)

Personal contact

Real-time service take-up

General services

Asynchronous service take-up

Learning transition
Service emphasis: *Academic and personal welfare support*
Including:
Academic information
Counselling
Personal welfare support
Cohort management
Rolling induction

Mid-career
Service emphasis: *Academic management*
Including:
Academic progression support and counselling
Student welfare services
Communication and support for students completing studies off-campus

Late-career
Service emphasis: *Academic and careers support*
Including:
Careers advice
Post-graduation destination advice and support
Financial advice
Academic support
Services for 'failing'/non-completing students

Graduation:
Service emphasis: *Administrative*
Including:
Careers advice
Provision of certification, references, etc.
General alumni information
Academic and welfare support for unsuccessful/continuing students (accommodation, finance, student counselling, family liaison)

Repatriation/immigration:
Service emphasis: *Careers support/alumni information*
Including:
Careers advice
Alumni information
Immigration and travel information
Repatriation counselling

Alumnus:
Service emphasis: *Communication/networking*
Including:
Careers advice
Alumni networks
Support for future recruitment
Graduate giving

2002a, b; Turner, 2006, a). Within this context, potential tensions between cross-border students and 'stay-at-home' service providers and peers require management, especially in the delivery of student services in newly internationalizing institutions. Historically, many HE support workers are very local – recruited from within the immediate locality of the institution – and those whose long-term experiences have been with the traditional student community: young, local students. Academic managers need to recognize the implications of this cultural balance in service provision and provide effective training and support to facilitate positive service relationships between local providers and their student 'customers'.

Infrastructure management

The management implications of a diversity of expectations and aesthetics held by students emerge in a range of related organizational areas. Institutions have rapidly recognized the need to upgrade student facilities, for example to take account of the expectations of premium fee-payers, including many cross-border students. Institutional infrastructure also needs to recognize these expectations in estates management and technological design. In general, institutional systems need to internationalize both communications and financial management infrastructure in order to minimize the stresses both on the systems themselves and on individual students. It is particularly important to manage information provision for students both before and after they arrive at the institution. Overall, 'active hosting' within the design and delivery of student services recognizes that cross-border students require a more integrated service offering than equivalent locals. The scope of their personal support and access is inevitably very narrow – with no family and friends locally to advise and help them and little or no pre-existing local knowledge. As a result, they rely to a much greater extent than their local peers on the institution to meet their needs, especially during the learning transition phase. Related to this, many distant families may seek information and perhaps involvement in decision making about a cross-border student's career, bringing a range of management and policy implications for institutions, especially in environments where the release of personal information is regulated by institutional policy or government legislation.

Internationalization at Home

Within the context of student diversity management, it is important to make active decisions about Internationalization at Home and Diversity strategies. Profound implications for programme recruitment policies and for the provision of basic services such as student accommodation exist, as we have discussed in previous chapters. The decisions are delicate. On the one hand, segregation of students into different groupings (international students, local students, mature students, etc.) may be discriminatory and can encourage active divisions between the groups because of their perceived differences. Equally, the planned integration of very diverse groups of students requires active management and support in order to anticipate the emergence of the inevitable differences in domestic and educational values and behaviour which will arise. Reports of tensions around student accommodation, attitudes to student alcohol use, the role of entertainment, sport and leisure activities within the study experience, for example, resonate in accounts about student experiences in cross-cultural university settings (Pritchard and Skinner, 2002; Turner, 2006a). The biggest challenge managerially and educationally in the management of student diversity, perhaps, is the acculturation of local students into recognizing HE as an intercultural learning and living space. Inevitably local students' perspectives will be informed by folkloric stereotypes of what it is to be a student within their local context. Institutions will need, therefore, to determine how far to construct institutional spaces as international or local and how to manage a range of student expectations within them.

Programmes

While many of the issues concerned with the management of staff and student diversity move across a diffuse range of areas within the scope of conventional university administration, programme diversity has tended to present an important and accessible face of HE internationalization to managers. Within the explosion of 'international' programme initiatives which have emerged in recent years, the most dominant route towards internationalization in many countries has been through direct recruitment of international students. Certainly the main thrust both of recruitment activity and government policy in the UK, for example, has been on overseas students coming directly to study to the UK, bringing with them useful economic and cultural contributions. The organization and management approach to such international recruitment has built upon institutions' existing operational bases and functioned – at least to some extent – within the existing institutional expectations. The demands that international students make on programme provision have functioned within a reasonably similar operations and administrative range to those provided for increasingly diverse local students, therefore, as we have discussed in Chapters 5 and 6.

At the same time, more novel forms of international programming have also been emerging, which are less well documented in the literature and which require different management responses. These include distance and open learning projects, where students may travel to the host country for short periods of time or study mainly through asynchronous technologically mediated means and of advanced standing arrangements where students study within an institution in their home country for part of the degree and then complete their studies in mainstream programmes in the host country. They also include Transnational Education projects and cross-border partnerships which are among the most novel of new forms of collaboration in which HE institutions have been engaging and which require a new set of organizational and management assumptions. Such projects involve the directly transacted delivery of all or part of award-bearing programmes in participating students' home countries, usually by a mixture of local and awarding-institution-based academics who work on the project for either short- or long-term teaching assignments. These programmes contrast with many of the more conventional forms of international education delivery. The student cohorts tend to be mono- rather than multicultural, for example. Staff teaching on the programmes are likely to come from highly international academic communities. Students also remain resident in their own local contexts, often continuing with their pre-existing social lives and activities. They study in a conventional class-room-based synchronous teaching and learning environment but within an educational context which is 'foreign'. The language medium for instruction is also often a second language for both students and some teachers. Organizationally, these projects represent complex international partnerships, involving diplomatic sensitivities negotiated with host governments to permit the award of foreign degrees on host country soil. As such they provide a strikingly different form of HE provision from many of the other modes of international cooperation and programming that exist and require support from complex, international management systems.

In spite of their growth in recent years, the regulatory environment for such projects continues to evolve and remains ambiguous. Transnational projects can suffer from a lack of distinctive quality assurance, even where they appear to be validated by a reputable international education provider. A survey of transnational projects across Asia identified a number of particular issues (Doorbar, 2004). The study identified that students engaged in transnational education projects were primarily motivated by career enhancement opportunities, were often mature students or had failed to win a place in the local university system. Many were financially unable to afford the cost of study overseas. As such, they constituted a different group from those typically recruited directly to overseas institutions. The study also found that transnational projects suffered from less strong recognition for the degree awards than either more established local or overseas provision, even where the validating institution was itself recognized. The general educational experience was not regarded as comparable with either the domestic mainstream or study overseas in a number of ways, such as language environment and strength of academic faculty. Local employers tended not to understand the degree award as readily as a domestic- or overseas-conferred degree. In general, both employer groups and students expressed reservations about a narrow profit-making emphasis within such projects and were concerned about their overall value for money. It seems clear, therefore, that transnational projects present particular management challenges, especially in securing both their status and educational quality. Such issues are compounded by the strategic complexities involved in what are often public-private partnerships, where overseas public universities engage in quasi-commercial partnerships with emerging domestic private education providers and where the legal and business context remains highly dynamic.

In spite of the structural and organizational issues surrounding transnational education in general, it is clear that this type of HE provides something distinctive for particular student constituencies, however, and possesses a number of useful teaching and learning characteristics (Naidoo, 2004; Chapman and Pyvis, 2005). During their development, transnational projects have tended to focus 'towards the needs of working life' (Tynjala *et al.*, 2003, p. 149), emphasizing vocational and applied subjects. In addition, transnational programmes also provide convenience, accessibility, high quality/ low cost. They show a strong customer focus and practical career-centred teaching in much of the programming. The key advantages of transnational education seem to be flexibility and familiarity. Programmes often allow students either part- and full-time study, and so are attractive to mature students, and those with family commitments. Additionally, the teaching and learning environment can be adapted to the specific needs of the mono-cultural cohort, as can academic support and programme delivery systems (Naidoo, 2004; Chapman and Pyvis, 2005).

In the context of international HE, transnational education is becoming more important and making particular contributions in environments such as China and India, where under-provision in key vocational and applied subjects remains acute and where government policies continues to encourage international exchange to underpin economic development. Transnational education remains characterized by ambiguity and considerable management complexity, however. Regulatory uncertainties, cross-border quality assurance issues, problems in achieving degree recognition from host country governments, and partnership difficulties as public and private sectors attempt to work together in a very dynamic environment, all contribute to the uncertain status of such projects. Their long-term viability is also open to question as domestic provision within host countries develops in both quality and quantity to meet local needs, taking advantage of local cultural fit in ways that are not open to international partnerships. While Transformative internationalization is dependant on multi-site programme delivery, therefore, the management challenges associated with transnational educational projects are significant and require highly skilled strategic integration into an institution's core long-term mission. Though their potential for international exchange and reciprocity is very high, they do not represent an easy route to the stabilization of international student fee revenues but are significant long-term educational ventures which have the potential to reshape the institutional orientation towards international engagement.

Managing the process of internationalization

International resourcing

In addition to the issues implied by the management of increasingly diverse human resources and programmes, one of the main stimuli towards internationalization, particularly within competitive orientations, has often been based on the revenue-earning potential that may be available from international student recruitment and the development of international educational partnerships. In previous chapters we have discussed the importance of hypothecated resource investment to support international partnerships, students and organizational development. Certainly internationalization implies a significant increase in the complexity of institutional resource management as people, revenues and physical resources move across borders. It is also clear that financial resource management issues provide one of the fulcra on which successful internationalization balances. In the UK context, for example, the Higher Education Policy Institute raised concerns in 2006 about the number of UK HEIs that were potentially vulnerable to the volatilities in international student recruitment markets because of the degree to which they have come to rely on international student fee income to underpin basic operating activities (HEPI, 2006). Similar concerns have been reported in other countries such as Australia which have been large receiving countries for international student migrants (Schapper and Mayson, 2004). Equally, cases from European nations adopting more cooperative orientations to internationalization have identified the resource intensity of investment in international activities and the long-term nature of that institutional spend (van der Wende, 2001; De Jong and Teekens, 2003). In general, therefore, the research literature indicates an environment in which internationalization has tended to encourage an imbalance in institutional resource management, with an overenthusiastic reliance on income generated from unstable revenue sources linked to an underprovision of skilled human resources and strategic investment to stabilize and support those income flows over the long term. Within the particular context of individual institutions, therefore, internationalization throws resource management into strong relief (Walters and Adams, 2001). As we have discussed above, student diversity in particular is driving strong expectations of the services and supports which institutions provide as part of the overall educational experience, implying significant resource impacts. Within Symbolic orientations towards internationalization, however, a lack of resource hypothecation and investment to support international activities is both consistent with the harnessing of international effort for the achievement of extrinsic business objectives and is also an indicator of its relatively volatile and potentially short-term character. On the other hand, within the Transformative orientation, strategic resourcing in support of internationalization is a clear priority for the institution. At either end of the spectrum, therefore, resource management issues are foregrounded and in particular the management of international revenue volatilities becomes an important management challenge.

Centralization versus decentralization

The implication of the historical development of internationalization and the iterations between individuals, institutions and policy-makers is that internationalization has developed as both an idiosyncratic, bottom-up movement as well as a top-down political and institutional movement. The shift of focus away from simple concerns of cross-border mobility is relatively recent. Acknowledgement of the requirement for institution-level strategic management for internationalization is also relatively new for many and brings implications not only for institutional financial strategies but also for external policy compliance, quality assurance systems, etc. At a practical level internationalization is something that requires structural management as well as presenting organizational challenges for the coordination of disparate university communities and the management of increasing campus cultural diversity. What seems clear, therefore, is that internationalization in culturally diverse settings demands the explicit integration of intercultural studies and intercultural communication into both the curriculum and the organizational systems of the institution:

> One must say that the intercultural and the international agenda have not yet, in every case, been integrated, but often rather lead a parallel existence. (Wachter, 2003, p. 8)

As internationalization becomes more developed, bringing more and more complex challenges to institutions, it tends to imply centralization which presents difficulties for many HEIs because of their traditionally devolved characters (Taylor, 2004). The complexities of internationalization management also imply increasing professionalization in management and administrative areas (Rodwell, 1998). Indeed, internationalization has been a key driver in the professionalization of HE management in the past 20 years as HEIs' operating environments have become more geographically and organizationally complex and dispersed. Professional international recruiters, admissions specialists and marketers have all swelled the ranks of traditionally low-key and conservative university administrators and introduced a much stronger administrative techno-structure into university management and organization (Peters, 2004). While inevitable as a response to the dynamics of international market operations, this shift has contributed to the realignment of power relations between university administration and academics (Churchman, 2006). Equally, the business emphasis of much of the internationalization thrust in many HEIs has intellectually distanced academic practitioners from it, leading to the development of potential tensions between the different tribes in the HE community with implications for the coherence and effectiveness of internationalization efforts:

> Although it is logical that what is embedded in policy and administrative systems should also be embedded and integral to the academic practices of an institution, this convergence is not always easy to achieve. (Leask, 2001, p.101)

Internationalization brings with it a number of significant strategic and organizational design issues which require long-term management initiative. Inevitably the particularities of institutional context will prompt a wide variety of responses to the dilemmas of management control and organizations. Nonetheless, the dynamics of the internationalization process, particularly where institutions are engaged in developing offshore, multi-channel programmes, staffed by workers with diverse contract types, imply an increase in tensions between centralizing and decentralizing forces within institutions. Such dilemmas are magnified where national and international validatory and quality control bodies are involved in institutional quality assurance for international programmes. Increases in the diversity of programmes and delivery points suggests a fragmentation of management controls, yet some evidence suggests that quality assurance systems, which are largely predicated along national or regional lines of accountability, tend to encourage both programme convergence and management centralization (Taylor, 2004). The management of the balance of power, therefore, both institutionally and at programme level, presents an important challenge in the face of increasingly reciprocal internationalization.

The influence of the international office

Since the 1980s in countries like the UK, USA and Australia dedicated international offices have developed and taken on an increasingly important role in HE internationalization. Their configurations can vary significantly from place to place. Sometimes they are narrowly tasked with an international student recruitment and institutional marketing role, sometimes more widely with responsibility for finding and managing international opportunities for academic collaboration or various kinds. In some environments the international office is responsible for a wide range of issues including international student welfare and the support of local students undertaking overseas study activities. In many cases, international offices take a key responsibility for the welcome and orientation for newly arriving international students. Managerially, directors of international offices are often in a key position in advising or determining institutional international strategies (Humfrey, 1999; Brockington, 2002). At the heart of their role, however, the marketing of the institution and recruitment of international students remains a dominant concern (Lambrech, 1998). Indeed, many international officers come from marketing and recruitment backgrounds rather than academic backgrounds – a trend that is increasing. Undoubtedly the role of the international office is highly influential over the style and orientation towards international engagement yet, surprisingly, the international office has received very little treatment in the literature. The particular marketing and recruitment emphasis to the work of international offices, linked to the professional orientation of the people who populate them, implies particular emphases to any strategy-making in which they might be involved and may go some way to accounting for the continuing competitive orientation to internationalization evident in many countries such as the UK and Australia (van der Wende, 2001). With recruitment in mind, target-setting for international offices can often become dominated by short-term considerations, moving from year to year with quantified targets articulated at institutional, departmental or even programme level for the participation of international students. Such a focus can also tend to build on the manifest demand for particular subjects of study, encouraging mass entry to business studies master's degrees, for example, rather than developing a broader focus. Their work also brings international offices into close contact with the commercial interface of international education, particularly in the form of private-sector student recruitment agents. Ethical questions about a reliance on commercial agents have arisen over a number of years (*Times Higher Education Supplement*, 2006d). At the same time, the complexities of long-distance recruitment in unfamiliar environments render their continued connection with HEIs almost inevitable. The particularities of this recruitment mode – agents' fee income largely derives from volumes of students placed rather than by necessarily determining the most appropriate educational fit – puts a strong emphasis on the commercial externalities of the recruitment process, particularly student numbers and fee levels rather than on a more balanced assessment of the match between applicant and institution. Reflecting this emphasis it is perhaps inevitable that concerns about such matters also become important to international officers and can colour their view of the commodification of international students and HE more generally.

International officers have been, perhaps, extremely successful at the job they were originally designated to do and have been able to bring extensive professional insights about the international environment into HEIs. International offices are often one of the key repositories of international knowledge resources available to institutional managers. Yet at the same time the basic scope and construction of that task prompts them towards commercialized, market-focused and competitive imaginings of the international environment. If the influence of international officers is central in the articulation of institutional strategy, it is unsurprising that strategy articulation adopts a sympathetic orientation towards competitive constructions of internationalization. It is important, therefore, while accepting the undoubted expertise of international offices in understanding the student market environment to balance this voice with other perspectives on international engagement in order to embrace the fullest opportunities for stable and sustainable internationalization and to temper the dominance of the market metaphor in management decision-making.

The embedded nature of internationalization

When approaching the management of internationalization it is important to reflect upon the transferability of best practice against the contribution of context and the essential embeddedness of internationalization within the particulars of local environments. As we discussed in the opening chapters, the notion of internationalization carries within it ideas about the importance of local context and national differentiation. Though useful management insights can be gained from the experience of other institutions, therefore, Transformative internationalization arises from the idiosyncratic interplay of the particular values and beliefs of individuals within institution and particular localities. The great temptation when responding managerially to internationalization may be to play towards the convergent forces of apparent globalization and marketization as much because their action seems palpable as anything else. Indeed, much of the emphasis in the practice literature contributes to the sense of internationalization as a dominantly convergent set of forces (Rodwell, 1998). Yet, as we have discussed, the implications of globalization are both unclear and complex. Market convergence can lead to short-termism and the emergence of non-reciprocal orientations.

Internationalization and marketization are neither an exclusive nor necessarily inevitable partnership. As with any institutional effort aimed at reflecting and directing the development of organizational culture, the management of internationalization usefully begins with the expression of the energies and conceptions of local institutional communities rather than the management imposition of external solutions on local conditions. Not only is this important in capturing the spirit of Transformative internationalization and setting fruitful conditions for long-term reciprocal international engagement, but at the same time it recognizes the cultural situatedness of knowledge construction and production, unifying management means and intellectual ends.

Within this context, it is also important to address the degree to which internationalization and international issues might be approached as a stand-alone strategic theme or integrated within the basic organizational work of the institution. To a large degree, this will depend on the international orientation emergent within individual institutions and their local environment. Nonetheless it is reasonably clear that within the context of Transformative institutions, internationalization is *both* embedded *and* provides an explicit strategic theme within organizational systems and planning. One of the key challenges within an institution which is actively internationalizing is to broaden institutional conceptions of internationalization away from the narrow, obvious focus on student and staff mobility and/or student recruitment, in order to enable more complex engagement and support the management of change across a range of basic organizational functions. In order to achieve this, the stimulation of a professional development-led normalizing discourse about internationalization seems a prerequisite, as we will discuss in Chapter 8. Nonetheless, the confinement of internationalization as a discrete institutional theme, somehow separated from the institutional mainstream, also brings its difficulties and has the potential to encourage deficit or accommodation approaches both to non-local people within university communities and also to conceptions of internationalization itself. It can also tend to endow internationalization with a sense of temporariness or short-termism, undermining its long-term strategic potential. In seeking to manage towards an embedded approach to internationalization, therefore, the interplay of explicit action and integration is delicate and dynamic, demanding a range of strategies which both broaden conceptions and engagement while focusing on practical action within narrower operational systems.

Internationalization and values management

One of the essential management challenges in the context of internationalization is the very difficult issue of values management. As we have discussed in previous chapters, particular orientations to internationalization are galvanized by the personal and intellectual values of people within institutional communities, which necessarily range across a broad spectrum. In addressing the management of institutional internationalization, therefore, academic managers must confront the need to acknowledge the influence that individuals' values might have on institutional direction. Central to this effort is professional and academic development, which we will discuss in more detail in the final chapter. Equally, however, managers need to make decisions about how to respond to those who do not support the institutional position on internationalization because: 'Knowledge will be resisted when it threatens familiar identities and unsettles the integrity of the self' (Carson, 2005, p.155). In some respects this is important to a far lesser degree within more Symbolic orientations. At this end of the internationalization continuum, individuals' personal and intellectual values are relevant only as far as they relate to the tangible business objectives which the institution is seeking from international effort rather than to internationalization itself. In this context, therefore, the manager's role is to articulate tangible business objectives and manage institutional activities towards their achievement in a conventional manner. Within Transformatively international institutions, however, the prompt towards internationalization derives iteratively from individuals and communities as well as institutional strategy.

Within complex organizations it is inevitable that some may not be as fully involved or committed to institutional aspiration as others. This is especially the case with Transformative internationalization because it embraces particular socially ethnorelative values which may not be universally shared within institutional communities and implies changes in academic work:

> As the internationalization process is incorporated in many different areas of the institution and for different purposes, different expectations, values, motivations and efforts from staff, students and other stakeholders, depending on their particular understandings of internationalization, emerge. The individual's personal and educational experiences, background, the work space they occupy and other environmental contexts are also influential . . . As the university diversifies, new rules and procedures need to

be established and, consequently, university workers must adjust their working practices – not always an easy process and different levels of resistance can be expected. (Meiras, 2004, pp. 376–8)

Even where basic values across the institution are broadly sympathetic, disciplinary norms may vary and implicit local pedagogies will also inform people's sense of what constitutes culturally inclusive practice and belief. For example, such difficulties may be compounded in research-intensive institutions if internationalization is closely allied to teaching and learning, as we will discuss in Chapter 8. Thus a series of bifurcations – teaching vs. research, institution vs. discipline, business vs. educational objectives, etc. – may coalesce to make some within institutional communities less able or willing to engage with internationalization. The long-term nature of Transformative internationalization inevitably involves extended participation, development and communicative effort to engage institutional people and address the impact of personal values on the process. Over time, therefore, the institutional orientation towards internationalization both grows and becomes clearer. New entrants will be able to understand the institutional positioning, as the process develops. It is essential at the earliest stages, however, to incorporate international issues transparently into human resource management and operational management systems and to facilitate extensive debate about international issues. Inevitably this work is likely only to shape behaviour and compliance with the accompanying risk of subversions and obstruction. Ultimately, it is probably only time, supportive professional development and employee turnover that could achieve a managed transition towards a more Transformative orientation.

Conclusion

Just as the impact of internationalization is wide-ranging across institutions, equally the management of internationalization presents a wide range of strategic and operational challenges. The central issues to emerge in the management context are that internationalization implies increasing management complexity and requires depth of skills in interpersonal and values management as well as within the conventional range of management and administrative tasks. Important strategic issues emerge about the design and organization of the management function itself and the responsiveness of nationally based systems of quality assurance and accountability to respond to the complexity and diversity of an internationally based operation. The volatility and dynamic nature of international engagement also imply the need for increasing management flexibility and the design and management of programmes and support services for students, academics and administrative workers. Such a volume of effort catalysed by the internationalization process might encourage a tendency towards increased centralization and management control over institutional operations. At the same time, increasing centralization risks undermining the long-term potential inherent in internationalization and the alienation of important groups within HE communities. One of the indications to emerge from the practice-based literature is that many institutions have embarked upon internationalization as the result of happenstance; recognition of its more fundamental impacts only after important strategic commitments have already been undertaken. Its development appears to be very much a trial and error process as institutions move from unidimensional constructions of internationalization towards more complex and contingent perspectives. In this context, the main emphasis in progress towards long-term sustainable international engagement seems to rely upon effective strategic management which is capable of responding to and orchestrating the local initiatives upon which internationalization is built. In order to achieve this, a key strategic management thrust is upon the development of people within HE communities, particularly academic workers who engage with internationalization within their routine activities. The management of academic development, therefore, is the focus of the final chapter.

Chapter 8

Internationalization, university teachers and academic development

Introduction: development-led internationalization

This chapter focuses specifically on professional development within internationalizing HEIs and explores some of the conceptual, organizational and structural issues that influence its design and delivery. Earlier, we have discussed a range of issues relating to academic and educational development and have suggested that the management of sustainable, transformative international engagement is highly dependant on the personal skills, values and commitment of individuals within HEI communities. This notion of internationalization foregrounds professional development as a key underpinning factor in its achievement. Whatever the overall impact of the internationalization phenomenon, however – at Symbolic or Transformative ends of the continuum – the debate implies profound practical academic development challenges, as university communities shift away from cultural homogeneity and mass internationalization embeds itself firmly in the institutional psyche (Peters, 2004).

Clearly, as we discussed in Chapter 7, internationalization stresses development needs for all groups of workers within HE communities, particularly support workers. The challenges of internationalization are both broad and relatively novel and have an impact on the basic systems and infrastructure of academies. Nonetheless, in management terms, the most significant groups within institutional communities are those who experience the greatest international exposure, primarily university teachers and other academic workers whose routine activities are undertaken in intercultural settings and with culturallydiverse groups of people. Academic workers are also one of the groups who appear most resistant to managed academic development initiatives and whose professional identity is undergoing profound changes in the light of educational internationalization (McWilliam *et al.*, 1999; Healey and Jenkins, 2003; Norton *et al.*, 2005). Since their contribution to Transformative internationalization is fundamental, therefore, discussion of professional development issues within this chapter is fixed on academic workers.

Development in internationalizing environments

Scope

One of the first development issues to address in the area of internationalization is in determining its scope and focus. Consistent with the emergence of literature addressing other aspects of HE internationalization, a body of professional development literature has emerged in recent years, exploring academic practices to enable university teachers to respond to cultural diversity among students. There is also a well-represented body of literature discussing intercultural teaching, learning and communication skills, which we have discussed in Chapters 4 and 5. Many of the themes from within this literature are echoed in Figure 8.1, which summarizes key development issues to have arisen from the discussions in earlier chapters. The aim of this chapter is not to articulate a particular content agenda for development programmes, however, but to consider the broader management and delivery issues associated with academic development that arise within an internationalizing environment. Its main objective is to suggest the need for a strategic reimagination of the role of academic development in embedding Transformative internationalization within HEIs.

Figure 8.1: Development for internationalization: some strategic themes

Skills: Cultural awareness, intercultural communication and competence in diverse professional settings
Management: Managing complex and diverse international organizations with dispersed multi-channel points of educational delivery; international resource management and international HRM, including managing workforce diversity
Diversity, engagement and participation: Development of disciplinary and cross-disciplinary communities of reciprocal practices to explore the implications of internationalization in different contexts
Curriculum: Development in support of embedding international perspectives and learning and teaching orientations into programming and curriculum
Academic practices: Development in cultural pedagogy and the implications of internationalization for constructions of teaching and learning and professional practices

Teachers and learners:
a focus within conventional professional development

Much of the thrust that emerges from the development and internationalization literature appears to draw on academic development mediated
through conventional professional development structures: primarily
through training courses or workshops offered by in-house academic
development service organizations. Leask (2005), for example,
discusses 'internationalization at the level of the teacher' in terms of
practical training in transactional skills and teaching competencies
delivered by development professionals. Indeed, the focus of initial
teacher education and academic development in HE has tended
to draw heavily on 'atheoretical' or craft-based constructions of
teaching, which lend themselves readily to a functional, training
style – fostering the development of 'generic' skills – while more
research-focused, critical 'educational expertise' approaches have
remained isolated from mainstream development efforts (Rowland,
2001). Such craft-based orientations to academic development derived
largely from the competency movement, popularized in the 1980s and
1990s, which maintains a strict focus on individuated development
and the transferable, skills-based aspects of the development task
(Manathunga, 2006). These approaches to the organization of
academic development can be effective, broad in their reach and
providing a good standardized starting-point from which individuals
can consider issues arising from their day-to-day working experiences.
In management terms, they are also reasonably discrete and relatively
accessible to design and deliver.

At the same time, such approaches have the tendency to close out
opportunities for wider discourse or deep intellectual engagement
with the social context in which teaching arises because of a focus on
behaviour rather than the values and beliefs which inform professional
practices (Trowler and Knight, 2000; Cranton and Caruscetta, 2002;
Norton *et al.*, 2005). Debates within the literature also highlight
the contribution of development practices to the persistence of local
folk pedagogies over more dynamic, research-informed orientations
(Trowler and Cooper, 2002; Blackwell and Blackmore, 2003).
Academic development practices that focus predominantly on skills,
therefore, have tended to reinforce an unreflective tradition in HE
teaching and learning practices owing to what is effectively a 'discourse
divorce' between developmental approaches adopted in respect of
disciplinary research practices and practical training in teaching:

Higher Education has suffered from a polarization between academic development which has tended to be pragmatic and practitioner based and pedagogical research which has, by and large, remained disassociated from actual practice. (Gosling, 2003, p. 72)

Internationalization and development

The adoption of skills-based development in internationalizing institutions can bring about particular unintended consequences. Bruch and Barty's analysis (1998), for example, identifies a range of possible orientations to institutional internationalization: Activity, Competency, Process and Organizational. They note that British HEIs have adopted primarily 'Activity'-based orientations, focusing on volumes of (revenue-generating) international initiatives at the expense of less tangible processual and systemic factors. They assert, however, that sustainable, long-term internationalization requires a more contingent multi-dimensional approach. Such broadly configured capabilities imply a qualitative focus on activities, linked to long-term, relationship-based actions to build enduring and sustainable international partnerships. They also note that an 'Activity' orientation also drives conventional 'training'-based academic development, focusing on tactical teaching skills and cultural awareness. Yet, they contend:

It is questionable how deep a contribution these activities, valuable in themselves, make to the internationalization of life on campus. Rather they largely represent a marginal degree of change leaving the bulk of the institution unaffected. (p. 27)

In this context it seems clear that attempting to support institutional internationalization through conventionally organized and delivered education or academic development initiatives may bring some initial benefits but may ultimately confine action within the frameworks of pre-existing local norms of practice rather than engendering the socially reflective learning and development that seems to be a prerequisite for long-term international sustainability.

Development towards an ethnorelative perspective

As we have proposed in the preceding chapters, Transformative internationalization is as much about values of international reciprocity within the institutional ethical and belief system as it is about skilful teaching and learning practices, requiring individuals to move from an ethnocentric to an ethnorelative position (Bennett, 1993; Yang, 2002; Gabb, 2006). In this context, the aim of the academic development effort must focus intimately on individuals' personal, social and professional values underlying the style with which they engage with cultural others:

> An important contemporary ethical issue arising in academic development is the place of tolerance towards others and to alternative systems of thought or belief. (Gosling, 2003, p. 70)

This is especially important in considering issues of cultural pluralism in diverse knowledge settings, where undiscussed issues can engender uneven power relations between members of a group or community. One of the key implications of internationalization for academic development, therefore, lies in the need to pluralize its governing assumptions in order to address such ethical questions appropriately. As well as the challenges to content, one of the inevitable consequences of a plural perspective attaches to the sense of stylistic definiteness encouraged by a competence-based approach to development. Gosling (2003), for example, suggests the ethical and philosophical value of provisionality or open-endedness in the context of academic development. Given the shifting dynamics of internationalization such an orientation seems appropriate and offers much as a vehicle for militating against the tendency to fix categories and stereotypes that is inherent in accommodation and deficit orientations. It also presents opportunities to pluralize understandings of knowledge systems, values and traditions in addition to behaviours and practices and integrates into notions of reflective practice and complex professional learning. One of the key obstacles to such an orientation, however, remains within the nationally defined benchmarks for university teacher education which fix notions of both academic practice and development into limited locally relevant historical categories that emphasize definite skills and behaviours.

Development and socially normative practices

A number of further drawbacks attend academic development activities organized with a focus on skills or competencies arising out of locally normative constructions of learning and learners. Educational development has tended historically to focus on universalistic notions of the educational experience, for example, and has proposed unitarist concepts of the meaning of 'learning', 'student' and 'teacher', etc., struggling to respond to the critical positioning of academic work within the HEI context (Trowler and Cooper, 2002). Rorty (1980), for example, reflects the dialectic posed to development to act simultaneously as a process of enculturation and to promote critical reflection of the dominant local discourse:

> Education has to start from acculturation. We can afford to question reality as a given only after have passed through stages of implicit and then explicit and self-conscious conformity to the norms of the discourses going on around us. (Rorty, 1980, p. 365)

In the context of internationalization, therefore, academic development needs to address the foundational philosophy of the disciplines and the particular academic context which is the subject of acculturation, exploring the implicit cultural assumptions at play within them. Moreover, relational or transacted constructions of HE pedagogy suggest that the styles of interaction involved in the learning process exert fundamental influence over the nature of the learning that takes place as well as being possessed of their own cultural baggage (Hamilton, 1999). In this analysis, teaching is neither neutral nor facilitative but is an emotional labour process and part of the construction of knowledge and its outcomes (Ogbonna and Harris, 2004). An academic development approach that does not explore the cultural as well as the cognitive implications of teaching styles is unlikely, therefore, to be able to support effective internationalization of classroom or curriculum:

> Teaching is as much about codes as it is about methods. Put another way, a code is a framework for practice, not a prescription of methods. (Hamilton, 1999, p. 148)

It is clear, therefore, that within an internationalizing environment, not only is it necessary to consider learning situations as socially constructed but that 'even the meaning of "learning" may be different within different social constructs' (Woodrow, 2001, p. 6). It is very important that academic development problematizes not only student and teacher learning styles but also explicitly addresses the socially constructed nature of learning itself if the teaching and learning interactions that take place in culturally diverse classrooms are to become inclusive. This may or may not imply a renegotiation of the concept of learning in international education. What it certainly does demand, however, is that HE teachers are equipped with both sufficient understanding of the cultural baggage within their own assumptions about professional practices and also are sufficiently interculturally sensitive to be able to make dominant local assumptions clear to non-local students. In this process, teachers need to be able to provide necessary formative experiences, not only so that non-local students can develop sufficient competency not to be disadvantaged against their local counterparts but to construct a learning space that is configured in an international manner, enhancing everyone's learning (Carroll and Ryan, 2005). Within the development process, it is very important, therefore, to reflect upon the cultural framing of academic practices, simultaneously exploring their disciplinary and pedagogic foundations. Internationalization of content within an ethnocentric pedagogy possesses inherent limitations in achieving inclusivity or open access. The key challenge for academic developers, therefore, is to work in a very broadly constructed manner rather than within the narrow confines of generic skills orientations which achieved locally valid teaching and learning competence.

In development terms, this is a tall order. Relatively little within the academic practice literature within the UK, for example, has discussed the practical implications of the social construction of learning for routine teaching practices and the cultural construction of classroom identities, even where issues of student domestic multiculturalism and international cultural diversity are addressed. The overwhelming focus of HE teacher education appears to have remained universalist, pluralizing content within a framework of remedially inclusive techniques for non-locals, while implicitly privileging local behavioural constructions of learning, students and teachers:

> The dialectic of culture and learning presents problems in that different societies (often unwittingly) misunderstand each other. On the macro level, it can create a mismatch between local subculture and that of the wider society within which that subculture exists, leading individual learners to a sense of dissonance or classroom unease. (Woodrow, 2001, p. 6)

> The strategies of teacher development are still basically limited to convincing teachers of the wisdom of reform and providing the necessary knowledge and skills that are thought necessary to enact change. These strategies are inadequate to the challenges of the deeply socially transformative change facing democratic societies in the 21st century . . . A language for attending to questions of identity is absent in these discourses of teacher development,

because they lack an explicit theory of the subject . . . we are left with simplistic notions of unitary identity and transcendent human nature. (Carson, 2005, p. 157)

What emerges from such analyses is a sense that cultural pluralism both as articulated within the teaching and learning and educational development literature has conventionally been boundaried by implicit pedagogic assumptions about academic practices and that much of the developmental focus has been upon addressing the recognition of student diversity rather than pluralizing academic practices themselves. The implication of this for academic development is that development activities can work to support the continuation of the deficit or accommodation approaches to academic practice even where they might seek to resolve it.

Teacher development, inclusivity and reciprocity

Arising from this discussion, it seems clear that teacher-student reciprocity in learning environments becomes an important sub-text for academic development. Broadly, the literature suggests that HE teachers may not have a clear sense of the learners' contexts and students' conceptions of learning, nor do they have a clear sense of educational theory (Teekens, 2003). Trigwell's (2003) analysis also identifies the centrality of teachers' prior experience and perception of the teaching situation as an influence on how teaching and learning happens. He identifies an understanding of five fundamental aspects that teachers need to bring to the classroom:

- Conceptions of teaching evoked
- Approaches to learning being adopted
- The learner's conceptions of learning
- The learner's perception of his or her learning environment
- What constitutes the space for learning for any particular topic

This is made more difficult in diverse teaching and learning settings where learners' conceptions of the teaching and learning space are so varied. One of the biggest implications for development for internationalization in teaching as it is transacted, therefore, is the embedding of ethnorelative interpersonal relations in the classroom. The developmental challenges posed by this requirement are clear. Fraser (2001), for example, recognized that Australian academic developers identified their task as changing the teaching tactics of academics but was not more widely couched in terms of considering the conditions that facilitate learning. In developing cultural inclusivity and understanding the implications of reciprocal internationalization, therefore, it is necessary to pluralize at the most basic level, embracing the legitimacy of different or alternative knowledge systems and attempting to defuse both inherently unitarist epistemological and pedagogical stances. The implications of this are significant. Not only is it not enough to consider conventional issues such as curriculum content and academic practices in the face of diversity, it is also essential to reconsider foundational philosophical academic frames of enquiry, styles of argumentation and the principles that legitimate classroom participation.

One of the key stepping-stones to achieving such deep, reciprocal approaches to academic development is to reconfigure university teachers as international and intercultural learners alongside their students. Given the rapidity of internationalization in many HE contexts, linked to the tendency to configure academic identity and development practices within intellectual rather than socio-cultural frames, it is not surprising that many commentators have objectified the learning focus exclusively on to students. Yet particularly in the context of Anglophone countries, which have shown a conscious focus on internationalization, many academics and university teachers' own experiences remain configured largely within their own cultural environment, as we have discussed in previous chapters. This inevitably poses challenges to development of an empathetic interpersonal orientation to internationalization. As Sanderson (2004) notes, this lack of international exposure tends to limit understanding of the implications of internationalization, driving reductionist colonial perspectives and engendering defensive, negative stereotypes about cultural others. One useful way, it seems, to gain an informed international perspective is to spend time living and working in an overseas environment, especially as a second-language speaker (Olsen and Kroeger, 2001; Trice, 2005). In a general sense, therefore, a key thrust within development for internationalization needs to be in engendering an understanding of intercultural issues from an experiential standpoint. It is in this context that teachers become intercultural learners alongside their students, engaged in a broad community of *reciprocal practices* which draw on broader frames of reference than those which are locally valid. We have discussed the practical career management issues implied by internationalization and staff diversity in Chapter 7. Inevitably, however, the international positioning of academic staff within the institution brings forth implications for the construction of power relations in and outside the classroom, requiring sensitive developmental and management processes. It also necessitates a definition of the development task away from simple skills or competency frameworks into broader perspectives integrating intellectual, affective and practical domains. Such an orientation also creates a learning space where international exchange is broadly inclusive, engaging both local and international groups of learners.

Development, values and teaching

Developmental orientations foregrounding the role of teachers' personal values and behaviours emerge in a number of commentaries about internationalization (Samuelowicz and Bain, 2001; Walker, 2004; Hills and Thom, 2005). Teekens (2003), for example, draws together clusters of characteristics in the profile of an 'ideal lecturer' for the international classroom:

1. Issues related to using a non-native language of instruction
2. Factors related to dealing with cultural differences
3. Specific requirements regarding teaching and learning styles
4. Insight into the cultural implications of using media and technology
5. Specific requirements connected with the academic discipline
6. Knowledge of foreign education systems
7. Knowledge of the international labour market
8. Personal qualities

and notes: 'Often teachers themselves do not enough reflect on their own roles and responsibilities in this highly complicated process' (p. 111).

In essence the above list articulates a useful agenda for the focus of academic development in the area of internationalization. It is important to note that it encompasses a range of disciplinary, pedagogic and personal areas that are not confined within 'teaching competence' models of professional development. Narrow constructions of internationalization articulated through a developmental emphasis on teaching skills underplay the holistic impact of internationalization on university life. This is particularly problematic in research-intensive universities, where teaching and learning concerns inhabit something of a 'Cinderella' status among many academics' priorities (Blackwell and Blackmore, 2003). Indeed, one of the main difficulties confronting internationalization is that its articulation within the HE context is so closely identified with teaching and learning issues. The literature suggests that some academics perceived internationalization as threatening to their research identities (Poole, 2001; Schapper and Mayson, 2004). Ultimately the association of internationalization with teaching and learning compounds the difficulty of incentivizing development in the HE context. Since teacher training in the university context is often patchy and often occurring in ad hoc, post-professional contexts, it is difficult to undertake a coherent approach to the international development task – more so if academics are unwilling to engage with professional identities that foreground teaching and learning alongside research:

> Most lecturers in higher education have little knowledge of educational theory. They teach their subject from experience, often based on how they were taught themselves. They assume that students understand the hidden messages of their teaching style . . . there is a potential danger that the international classroom will become elitist. (Teekens, 2003, p. 115)

Implementation issues

Development, compliance and commitment

As we have suggested at various points, winning intellectual engagement from academics to the professional changes implied by high levels of internationalization – 'existential internationalization' (Sanderson, 2004) – is an essential component of effective intercultural development (Webb, 2005):

> Significant change and development in how we understand and practise teaching in higher education will only occur through deep and transformative learning experiences in which the faculty member is substantially engaged in a problem they care about. (Light, 2003, p. 153)

A focus on skills and knowledge-based development, therefore, may well enable university communities to become behaviourally *compliant with* institutional commitments to greater international reciprocity but marginalize academics' personal and intellectual *commitment to* the institutional agenda, which of necessity requires a different, critical-discursive approach to the development task (Turner and Robson, 2007). Indeed, much academic development in the area of internationalization to date has evolved to help staff with the 'problems' of international students rather than to internationalize the services themselves' (Bruch and Barty, 1998, p. 27). Such approaches maintain deficit or accommodation characterizations of non-local students, limiting opportunities for the development of positive reciprocal international engagement (Biggs, 2003). Balancing institutional requirements for effective intercultural development through a conventional training-type focus, therefore, may well prove problematic.

The organizational role of professional development

A further issue that may preclude academics' engagement with internationalization is their relationship with academic developers. The academic development literature identifies long-standing debates about the credibility of professional developers in attempting to provide support for academic colleagues (Rowland *et al.*, 1998; Rowland, 2002; Trowler and Cooper, 2002; Manathunga, 2006). Partly this stems from the way in which academic development functions have been designed institutionally – as central services, similar in style and function to corporate staff training units. Such units are tasked with a variety of potentially conflicting responsibilities involving the provision of practical induction and skills training for various staff groups as well as more complex activities involving academic development:

> The obvious tensions between supporting managerial 'top-down' initiatives and the needs or wishes of 'ordinary' staff mean that academic developers can sometimes feel like either the filling in a sandwich or as a cushion between conflicting interests. (McDonald, 2003, p. 9)

Within many institutions, relatively little scope is provided for development professionals to become or remain research active within their field (Rowland, 2001). Career and developmental paths for professional developers in HEIs are also unclear:

> There are some significant issues about standards, preparation and training which underlie issues of capacity and capability. (Blackwell and Blackmore, 2003, p. 12)

We have proposed that Transformative internationalization is primarily development-led or at the very least foregrounds academic development as a means of embedding 'existential internationalization' within institutions. Yet the lack of professionalization and unclear status of academic developers in the institutional scheme reduces opportunities to manage internationalization through the vehicle of development. In this context it is important to recognize the strategic contribution of academic development to internationalization, adopting a generally open and investment-focused perspective in respect of long-term rewards (Blackwell and Blackmore, 2003). Flowing from the divergent institutional objectives set for them, developers' preoccupations can seem somewhat removed from those of the disparate client groups with whom they come into professional contact, however (Stefani and Matthew, 2002; McAlpine, 2006). This may be particularly the case with academic staff, whose teaching work aligns quite closely to the primary concerns of academic developers but who carry out this work within a disciplinary, research-based context. Academic staff are essentially predisposed to operate within a critical, discourse-based teaching and learning framework rather than one that is functional, skills- or competency-focused – the conventional institutional focus ascribed for developers (Trowler and Knight, 2000; Akerlind, 2005).

Inevitably, therefore, differences in style can occur when approaching a development or teaching task which confronts academics with institutional development activities. As Blackwell and Blackmore note (2003), for staff development units in HEIs to work successfully, they require certain conditions:

- Autonomy to act
- To adopt partnership approaches designed to serve 'top', 'middle', and 'bottom' interests
- They need to be sensitive to the cultures of disciplines
- Visible and sustained leadership support
- To be led by people who can gain the trust of everyone in the university

In terms of development for internationalization, therefore, the biggest issue for developers is that they are enabled to simultaneously serve organizational strategy and the interests of the various constituencies in the university staff community. This is likely to become problematic where management approaches to internationalization and liberal academic internationalist values do not align.

Professional and disciplinary cultures

A further issue confronting the design and delivery of institutional development activities is the tribal power of the disciplines which has been well documented in the HE literature (Becher and Trowler, 2001). Healey and Jenkins (2003), for example, indicate the divergence in basic constructions of development held by academics and developers respectively:

> For most academic staff *academic* development is primarily about staff being scholars (and perhaps 'active' researchers) in a discipline per se. (p. 47)

Such a notion contrasts both the craft-based view that academics take of their teaching role and with the professionalization and skills orientation conventionally adopted by academic developers. Healey and Jenkins also argue the centrality of disciplines as an organizational unit for development because of the boundaries and differences inherent within the disciplinary frame. One of the key benefits in development for internationalization is the inherently international nature of many disciplinary networks, though the generic nature of much academic development work has tended to underplay its contribution. Gosling (2003) echoes the focus on the important contribution of disciplinary-based development:

> An important part of the value-set embodied in a discipline is the way in which the discourse of the subject values or denies value to certain sorts of knowledge claims and certain sorts of argument. The extent to which the teacher should make explicit these value commitments is a contentious matter. (p. 73)

Other commentators (Akerlind, 2005; Warhurst, 2006) make an account of the important contribution of the disciplines in developing the social, dialogic learning and development that is essential in the communication of disciplinary values and norms to new entrants. They suggest that the professional cultures of disciplines possess an important role in enculturation, cultural development and in setting and legitimizing disciplinary boundaries. Disciplinary groups are therefore the locus for the majority of social and informal learning for academics (Warhurst, 2006). Given the challenges to conventionally organized formal academic development in embedding international or ethnorelative perspectives, much of the focus for academic development lies within the informal, social learning that takes place within disciplinary communities of practice. At the same time, we have already discussed the socially and intellectually normative tendencies of such local communities. In order to harness the developmental opportunities within disciplinary communities, therefore, academic developers have a potentially powerful role as cross-disciplinary and cross-cultural facilitators or brokers.

Development dilemmas

Emerging from the preceding discussion, the central challenges for academic developers in the area of internationalization are essentially threefold. Firstly, the strategic importance of internationalization to institutions is clear – international student revenues have come to underpin basic operating functions within HEIs in many countries, for example. The obvious starting-point from which institutions might initiate development activities is by utilizing existing academic development service providers. Consequently senior managers have put considerable pressure on academic developers to support internationalization and bring skills and commitment to that end. Secondly, as noted above, the development of intercultural 'competencies' are as much about attitudes and values as about skills, yet long-standing debates suggest that, while conventional development activities can work effectively to support knowledge and skills, personal values and attitudes are less open to such interventions. Thirdly, stylistic differences in defining the nature of the teaching and/or development task make it difficult for professional developers to work effectively with research-focused academics in this area. Taken together, these three issues stress the importance for academic developers to adopt an independent brokerage role within institutions which can address the challenges and contradictory demands made of them. They also suggest the need for a broad rearticulation of both the conceptual and professional boundaries around academic development activities and a reconfiguration of roles, and means of intervention within institutional and disciplinary communities (McAlpine, 2006).

Many institutional case studies illustrate the importance of the values-based aspects of intercultural development as a contributor to deep or Transformative internationalization (Egege and Kutieleh, 2003; Crabtree and Sapp, 2004; Andres, 2005; Golz, 2005; Major, 2005). In spite of numerous accounts of interculturally competent practices, nonetheless a generally negative view of internationalization emerges from much of the literature and identifies defensive postures as local practices and norms are perceived as under threat. A clear strategic imperative exists, therefore, in the employment of academic development as a key tool in winning engagement of people within HEI communities, as well as achieving its more practical objectives. Given the defensive style which characterizes much of the discourse about academic identity and managerialism in general and particularly colouring accounts about the impact of globalization and internationalization on local educational practices, academic development emerges as a key catalyst in achieving either support from or alienation of academic groups within HE communities. Again, a primary variable here appears to be stylistic – where development practice emphasizes the professionally critical and organizationally consultative in discussions about professional matters, potential synergies between the positive engagement of academic workers and institutional interests emerge. Where the participative aspects of development are closed out within a skills-competency agenda, however, the potential for disengagement also seems high. In general this resonates with the wider difficulties associated with remedial or deficit orientations towards both internationalization and to academic development. In effect, by mutual association, they compound their potential for negative unintended consequences. Where internationalization is approached as a narrow gateway – particularly where that gateway is sign-posted with the language of competition or globalization – tensions of convergence and conformity inevitably marginalize or alienate some members of diverse institutional communities. By widening the portal through the means of broadly constructed academic development, positive opportunities proliferate. Within this context, therefore, one of the key challenges for academic managers is to broaden the emphasis of the development effort, mindful of the crucial influence of both affective and cognitive schema on behavioural changes.

Conclusion: responding to the development dilemmas?

The discussion in this chapter suggests that conventional approaches to the organization of institutional academic development, linked to the practice-based assumptions governing its practice, may struggle to support the emergence of Transformative internationalization. In some cases, narrowly constructed orientations which regard academic development as a remedy for teaching and learning skills deficits might actually encourage convergence on exclusive local practices and therapeutic attitudes to learning diversity. Yet at the same time people, their values, beliefs and behaviours are central to the ethnorelative shift that is inherent in deep and sustainable internationalization. Appropriate academic development is an important strategic tool for academic managers within internationalizing institutions, therefore.

Of essential importance in this context is the design and organization of the academic development function and the aims and objectives which are set for it. Key questions apply to the professional identity and role of developers, their focus of attention, the design of development initiatives and the determination of those who are included in the development effort. Certainly the continuing polarization between practical academic development, pedagogic researchers and academics in disciplines seems only to obstruct effective development and the realization that values, beliefs and skills need to align in order to embrace the fullest potential inherent within internationalization.

One obvious answer to this difficulty, at which the development literature hints, lies in the managed combination of conventional 'atheoretical' development activities together with research-based 'educational expertise' (Rowland, 2001; Fraser, 2006). Such partnerships have the potential to harness opportunities for critical, research-based social learning as well as more conventional development. Partnership approaches would work to integrate the delivery of appropriate skills-based development activities with research-led discourse, conferencing activities and the sponsorship and dissemination of HE research within institutions. As shown in Figure 8.2, the potential for the combination is powerful. Not only capturing the opportunity to inculcate both the competence and commitment necessary for long-term, reciprocal international engagement, it would also help academics to find the reflective and social developmental space which the literature indicates as important in achieving successful change.

Adopting this approach would require HEIs to explicitly distribute responsibility for development between teachers, education researchers and professional developers. Precedents for such a sharing of responsibility for formal development exist but are not widespread and tend to be informal, focusing on loose, spontaneous sharing between developers and researchers. Few examples exist of a coordinated organizational strategy which adopts a research-based orientation to routine academic development. Ultimately, however, the greatest challenge confronting HEIs when embedding effective internationalization is one of definition and focus. Within a competitive, market-oriented mindset it seems easy to construct internationalization as a practical 'fact of life' to be accepted by everyone and to focus on the more obvious aspects accompanying it – primarily the need to equip university staff with skills to enable them to cope with international diversity. By doing so, however, institutions miss the underlying social-values aspects underpinning internationalization. After all, being sufficiently skilled at working with diverse groups of students or colleagues does not necessarily imply willingness to do so or to make others feel welcomed to and involved in the university community. The essence of HE internationalization is both about crossing cultures and reflecting on local cultural certainties in the light of new insights. Crossing the more porous boundaries of professional cultures to create institutional partnerships and a shared understanding about the implications of internationalization, to develop dialogue about similarities and differences of values and practices, seems an appropriate model, therefore, with which to approach the challenges of internationalization.

Figure 8.2: The role of reflective academic development partnerships in internationalizing university teachers: combining competence and commitment

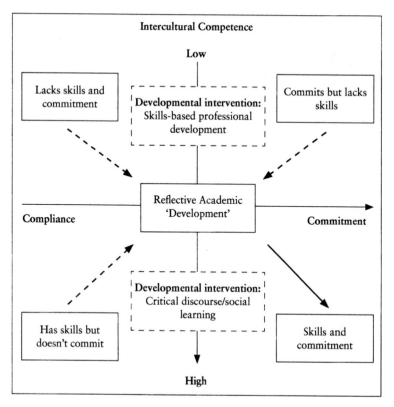

References and selected bibliography

Ackers, Jim (1997), 'Evaluating UK courses: the perspective of the overseas student', in McNamara, David and Harris, Robert (eds), *Overseas Students in Higher Education: Issues in Teaching and Learning*. London: Routledge, 187–200.

Adams, K. (2004), 'Modelling success: enhancing international postgraduate research students' self-efficacy for research seminar presentations'. *Higher Education Research and Development*, 23 (2): 10–26.

Adrian-Taylor, S.R., Noels, K.A. and Tischler, K. (2007), 'Conflict between international graduate students and faculty supervisors: towards effective conflict prevention strategies'. *Journal of Qualitative Studies in Education*, 11: 90–117.

Akerlind, Gerlese, S. (2005), 'Academic growth and development – how do university academics experience it?'. *Higher Education*, 50: 1–32.

Altbach, P.G. (1989a), 'The new internationalism: foreign students and schools'. *Studies in Higher Education*, 14: 125–36.

— (1989b), 'Twisted roots: the western impact on Asian higher education'. *Higher Education*, 18: 9–30.

Althen, G. (ed) (1994), *Learning across cultures*. Washington, DC: NAFSA.

American Council on Education (ACE) (2000), *Preliminary status report: internationalizationof US higher education*. www.acenet. edu/bookstore.

— (2005), *By the numbers: International student enrolment in US colleges and universities declines*. www.acenet.edu/AM/Teamplate. cfm?section.home.

— (2007), www.acenet.edu/Content/NavigationMenu/ ProgramsServices/International/index11.htm.

Andere, Eduardo (2004), 'The international higher education market: Mexico's case'. *Journal of Studies in International Education*, 8(1), 56–85.

Anderson, L.W., Krathwohl, D.R., Baron J.B. and Sternberg, R.J.

(eds) (2001), *Teaching Thinking Skills: Theory and Practice*. New York: Freemann.

Andres, Ian (2005), 'Transformation in education: the intercultural agenda of internationalizing teacher education – a Canadian perspective', in Golz, Reinhard (ed), *Internationalization, Cultural Difference and Migration: Challenges and Perspectives of Intercultural Education*. London, Transaction Publishers, 137–46.

Angelil-Carter, S. (2000), *Stolen Language? Plagiarism in Writing*. Harlow: Pearson Education.

Angus, Lawrence (2004), 'Globalization and educational change: bringing about and shaping and re-norming of practice'. *Journal of Education Policy*, 19: 23–41.

Aoki, K. (2005), 'Japanese higher education institutions in the 21st century – the challenge of globalization and internationalization'. *Electronic Journal of Contemporary Japanese Studies*, Discussion Paper 7, 4 November.

Archibong, U. (1995), 'Overseas students' research supervision: their experiences and expectations', *Journal of Graduate Education*, 1: 85–93.

Argyris, C. and Schon, D. (1978), *Organizational Learning: a Theory of Action Perspective*. Reading, MA: Addison-Wesley.

— (1992), *Organizational Learning II: Theory, Method and Practice*. Reading, MA: Addison-Wesley.

Asmar, C. (2001), 'A community on campus: Muslim students in Australian universities', in Saeed, A. and Akbarzadeh S. (eds), *Muslim Communities in Australia*. Kensington: UNSW Press.

— (2004), *Cultural difference in western universities: intercultural and internationalized responses to a changing world*. Paper to ISL conference, Birmingham, September 2004.

— (2005), 'Internationalising students: reassessing diasporic and local student difference'. *Studies in Higher Education*, 30(3), 291–305.

Asteris, Michael (2006), 'British universities: the "coal exporters" of the 21st century'. *Studies in International Education*, 10(3), 224–40.

Astiz, Fernanda, Wiseman, Alexander W. and Baker, David P. (2002), 'Slouching towards decentralization: consequences of globalization for curricular control in national education systems'. *Comparative Education Review*, 46(1): 66–88.

Australian International Education Foundation (1998), *International Skills for Young Australians*. Canberra: Australian Government Publishing Service.

Australian Vice-Chancellors' Committee (2000), *Key Statistics: Access on Australian Universities*. www.avcc.edu.au.

— (2001). *AVCC discussion paper on international education.* Canberra.

AUT/DEA (Association of University Teachers and Development Education Association) (1999), *Globalisation and Higher Education: Guidance on Ethical Issues Arising from International Activities.* www.dea.org.uk/publication-cd96a1ba9949220640e8f5 6dbb4132.

Back, K., Davis, D. and Olsen, A. (1996), *Internationalisation and higher education: Goals and strategies.* Canberra: Australian Government Publishing Service.

Bada, M.M. (1994), 'Greek women's roles in postgraduate studies in Britain'. Unpublished MSc dissertation, cited in Leonard, D. and Morley, L. (2003), *The Experiences of International Students in UK Higher Education: a Review of Unpublished Research.* London: Institute of Education, University of London.

Badley, G. (2000), 'Developing globally competent university teachers', *Innovations in Education and Training International,* 37 (3): 244–53.

Bamford, J., Marr, T., Pheiffer, G. and Weber-Newth, I. (2002), 'Some features of the cultural and educational experience and expectations of international postgraduate students in the UK'. BEST Conference, 9 April 2002: Supporting the Teacher: Challenging the Learner. www.66.102.1.104/scholar?h1=en& 1r=&q=cache:Zah7INjEzXYJ:www.business.ltsn.ac.uk/events/ BEST%25202002/Papers/Weber-Newth.PDF+Bamford+et+al,+(20 02)+international+students+.

Bandura, A. (1977), *Social learning theory.* Englewood Cliffs, NJ: Prentice Hall.

Banks, J. (1999), *An introduction to multicultural education.* Boston, MA: Allyn and Bacon.

Barker, John (1997), 'The purpose of study: attitudes to study and staff-student relationships', in McNamara, David and Harris, Robert (eds), *Overseas Students in Higher Education: Issues in Teaching and Learning.* London: Routledge, 108–24.

Barnett, R. (1997), *Higher Education: a critical business.* Buckingham: Society for Research into Higher Education/Open University Press.

— (2000), *Realizing the University in an age of supercomplexity.* Buckingham: SRHE/Open University Press.

Bartell, Martin (2003), 'Internationalization of universities: a university culture-based framework', *Higher Education,* 45: 43–70.

Batelaan, Pieter and Gundare, Ieva (2000), 'Intercultural education, co-operative learning and the changing society'. *Intercultural Education,* 11: 31–4.

Bayley, S., Fearnside, R., Arnol, J., Misiano, J. and Rottura, R. (2002), 'International students in Victoria'. *People and Place*, 10 (2): 45–54.

Beazely, K.C. (1992), *International education in Australia through the 1990s*. Canberra: Australian Government Publishing Service.

Becher, Tony and Trowler, Paul R. (2001), *Academic Tribes and Territories: Intellectual Enquiry and the Cultures of Disciplines*. Buckingham: SRHE/Open University Press.

Beekhoven, S., de Jong, U. and van Hout, H. (2003), 'Different courses, different students, same results? An examination of differences in study progress of students in different courses'. *Higher Education*, 46: 37–59.

Bekhradnia, Bahram (2006), *Demand for HE to 2020*. Higher Education Policy Institute. www.hepi.ac.uk/pubs. asp?DOC=Reports.

Bekhradnia, Bahram and Sastry, Thomas (2005), *Brain Drain: Migration of Academic Staff to and from the UK*, Higher Education Policy Institute. www.hepi.ac.uk/pubs.asp?DOC=Reports.

Bell, M. (2005), *Internationalising the higher education curriculum – Do academics agree?* www.herdsa.org.au/conference2004/ Contributions/RPapers/P036-jt.pdf.

Bennell, B. and Pearce, T. (2003), 'The internationalization of higher education: exporting education to developing and transitional economies'. *International Journal of Educational Development*, 23: 215–32.

Bennett, J.M. (1986), 'Modes of cross-cultural training: conceptualizing cross-cultural training as education. *International Journal of Intercultural Relations* (IJIR), 102: 117–34.

Bennett, J.M. and Bennett, M.J. (2004), 'Developing intercultural sensitivity: an integrative approach to global and domestic diversity', in Landis, D., Bennett, J.M. and Bennett, M.J. (eds), *Handbook of Intercultural Training* (third ed.), Thousand Oaks, CA: Sage, 147–65.

Bennett, M.J. (1993), 'Towards ethnorelativism: a developmental model of intercultural sensitivity', in Paige, R.M. (ed.), *Education for the Intercultural Experience*. Yarmouth, ME: Intercultural Press, 21–72.

Berger, J. (2000) 'Optimizing capital, social reproduction, and undergraduate persistence', in Braxton, J. (ed.), *Reworking the Student Departure Puzzle*. Nashville, NT: Vanderbilt University Press, 95–126.

Bhabha, H.K. (1994), *Location of Culture*. London and New York: Routledge.

Bhawuk, D.P.S., and Triandis, H. C. (1996), 'The role of culture theory in the study of culture and intercultural training', in Landis, D. and Bhagat, R.S. (eds), *Handbook of intercultural training* (2nd edn), Thousand Oaks, CA: Sage, 17–34

Biggs, J. (1994), 'Asian learners through Western eyes: an astigmatic paradox', *Australian and New Zealand Journal of Vocational Educational Research*, 2(2): 40–63.

— (1996), 'Enhancing teaching through constructive alignment'. *Higher Education,* 32(3): 347–64.

— (1999), *Teaching for Quality Learning at University: What the Student Does.* Buckingham: Society for Research into Higher Education and Open University Press.

— (2003), *Teaching for Quality Learning at University: What the Student Does* (2nd edn, Maidenhead: Open University Press.

Black, K (2004), *Review of Factors Which Contribute to the Internationalisation of a Programme of Study.* www.hist.ltsn. ac.uk/johiste.

Blackmore, Paul and Blackwell, Richard (2003), 'Academic roles and relationships', in Blackwell, Richard and Blackmore, Paul (eds), *Towards Strategic Staff Development in Higher Education.* Buckingham: Open University Press.

Blackstone, T. (2004), 'Staying attractive'. *Guardian,* 9 March.

Blackwell, Richard and Blackmore, Paul (2003), 'Setting the scene: rethinking strategic staff development', in Blackwell, Richard and Blackmore, Paul (eds), *Towards Strategic Staff Development in Higher Education.* Buckingham: Open University Press.

Bleiklie, Ivar and Powell, Walter, W. (2005), 'Universities and the production of knowledge – introduction'. *Higher Education,* 49(1): 1–8.

Bolton, G. (2005), 'Taking responsibility for our stories: in reflective practice, action learning and Socratic dialogue'. *Teaching in Higher Education,* 10(2): 271–80.

Bond, S. (2003), *Untapped Resources, Internationalization of the Curriculum and Classroom Experience: A Selected Literature Review.* Ottawa: Canadian Bureau for International Education.

Borland, H and Pearce, A. (2002), 'Identifying key dimensions of language and cultural disadvantage at university'. *Australian Review of Applied Linguistics,* 25 (2): 101–27.

Bourdieu, P, (1996), *The State Nobility.* Cambridge: Polity Press.

Bourdieu, P. and Passeron, J. (1990), *Reproduction in Education, Society and Culture.* London: Sage.

— (1996), 'Introduction: Language and the relationship to language in the teaching situation', in Bourdieu, P., Passeron, J-C. and De Saint

Martin, M., *Academic Discourse: Linguistic Misunderstanding and Professorial Power*. Cambridge: Polity Press.

Boyle, B., White, D. and Boyle, T. (2004), 'A longitudinal study of teacher change: what makes professional development effective?' *The Curriculum Journal*, 15: 45–68.

Braddock, R., Roberts, P., Zheng, C. and Guzman, T. (1995), *Survey on Skill Development in Intercultural Teaching of International Students*. Sydney: Macquarie University, Asia Pacific Research Institute.

Bradley, Harriet, Erickson, Mark, Stephenson, Carrol and Williams, Steve (2000), *Myths at Work*. Oxford: Polity Press.

Braine, George (2002), 'Academic literacy and the nonnative speaker graduate student'. *Journal of English for Academic Purposes*, 1: 59–68.

Bremer, L. and van der Wende, M. (eds) (1995), *Internationalising the Curriculum in Higher Education: Experiences in the Netherlands*, The Hague: The Netherlands Organisation for International Co-operation in Higher Education.

Bretag, T. (2006), 'Developing "third space" interculturality using computer-mediated communication'. *Journal of Computer-Mediated Communication*, 11(4), article 5. jcmc.indiana.edu/vol11/issue4/bretag.html.

Bretag, T., Horrocks, S. and Smith, J. (2002), 'Developing classroom practice to support NESB students in information systems courses: some preliminary findings'. *International Education Journal*, 3(4): 57–69.

Brew, A. (2002), 'Research and the academic developer: a new agenda'. *International Journal for Academic Development*, 7: 112–22.

— (2003), 'The future of research and scholarship in academic development', in Eggins, Heather and McDonald, Ranald (eds), *The Scholarship of Academic Development*. Buckingham: Open University Press, 165–81.

Brew, A. and Peseta, T. (2004), 'Changing postgraduate supervision practice: a programme to encourage learning through reflection and feedback'. *Innovations in Education and Teaching International*, 41(1): 5–22.

British Council (2007), *Overview of the Prime Minister's Initiative*. www.britishcouncil.org/eumd-pmi-overview.htm.

British Council, Educational Counselling Service (2000), *Realising our Potential: a Strategic Framework for Making UK Education the First Choice for International Students*. Manchester: The British Council.

Brockington, Joseph (2002), 'Moving from international vision to institutional reality: administrative and financial models for education abroad at liberal arts colleges'. *Journal of Studies in International Education*, 6(3): 283–91.

Brown, David. K. (2001), 'The social sources of educational credentialism: status cultures, labour markets and organizations'. *Sociology of Education*, 74: 19–34.

Brown, Ken (1998), *Education, Culture and Critical Thinking*. Aldershot: Ashgate.

Brown, J. and Duguid, P. (1991) 'Organisational learning and communities of practice: towards a unified view of working, learning and innovation.' *Organizational Science*, 2(1): 40–57.

Brown P. and Scase, R. (1994), *Higher Education and Corporate Realities*, London: UCL Press.

Bruch, Tom and Barty, Alison (1998), 'Internationalizing British higher education: students and institutions', in Scott, Peter (ed) *The Globalization of Higher Education*. Buckingham: Open University Press, 18–31.

Bruner. J. (1996), *The Culture of Education*. Cambridge, MA: Harvard University Press.

— (1999), 'Folk pedagogies', in Leach, Jenny and Moon, Bob (eds), *Learners and Pedagogy*. London: Sage, 4–20.

Burbules, N.C. and Torres, C.A. (2000), *Globalization and Education: Critical Perspectives*. New York: Routledge.

Burke, Rachel (2006), 'Constructions of Asian international students: the "Casualty" model and Australia and "Educator"'. *Asian Studies Review*, 30: 333–54.

Busher, H. (2001), 'Being and becoming a doctoral student: culture, literacies and self-identity'. Paper presented to TESOL Arabia Conference, Dubai Women's College, Dubai, UAE, 14–16 March.

Butcher, A. (2000). 'International students and the internationalisation of education in Australia and New Zealand'. *Norrag News*, 27: 12–15.

Butcher, Andrew and McGrath, Terry (2004), 'International students in New Zealand: needs and responses'. *International Education Journal*, 5(4): 540–51.

Butler, D. (1998), 'Promoting self-regulation in the context of academic tasks: the strategic content learning approach'. Paper presented at the August 1998 meeting of the American Psychological Association, San Francisco.

Cadman, K. (2000), 'Voices in the air: evaluations of the learning experiences of international postgraduates and their supervisors'. *Teaching in Higher Education*, 5(4): 475–91.

Cameron, Lynne and Low, Graham (eds) (1999), *Researching and Applying Metaphor*. Cambridge: Cambridge University Press.

Camiciotolli, Belinda Crawford (2005), 'Adjusting a business lecture for an international audience: a case study'. *English for Specific Purposes*, 24: 183–99.

Canning, J. (2007), 'Pedagogy as a discipline: emergence, sustainability and professionalization'. *Teaching in Higher Education*, 12(3): 393–403.

Carnoy, Martin and Rhoten, Diana (2002), 'What does globalization mean for educational change? A Comparative Approach'. *Comparative Education Review*, 46(1): 1–9.

Carroll, J. (2002), *A Handbook for Deterring Plagiarism in Higher Education*. Oxford: Oxford Centre for Staff and learning Development.

Carroll, Jude and Ryan, Janette (2005a), '"Canaries in the Coalmine": International Students in Western Universities', in Carroll, Jude and Ryan, Janette (eds), *Teaching International Students: Improving Learning for All*. London: Routledge, 3–12.

Carroll, Jude and Ryan, Janette (eds) (2005b), *Teaching International Students: Improving Learning for All*. London: Routledge.

Carson, Terry (2005), 'Becoming somebody different: teacher identity and implementing socially transformative curriculum', in Golz, Reinhard (ed.), *Internationalization, Cultural Difference and Migration: Challenges and Perspectives of Intercultural Education*. London: Transaction Publishers, 153–8.

Caruana, V. (2004), 'International mission impossible? ICT and Alternative approaches to internationalising the curriculum'. Networked Learning Conference, Symposium 3, Sheffield. www. networkedlearningconference.org.uk/past/nlc2004/proceedings/ symposia/symposium3/caruana.htm.

Caruana, V. and Hanstock, H.J. (2003), *Internationalising the Curriculum: From Policy to Practice*. www.ece.salford.ac.uk/ proceedings/papers/vc_03.rtf.

— (2005), 'Internationalising the curriculum – at home or far away? Making connections through a holistic approach based on inclusivity'. www.edu.salford.ac.uk/scd/ltprac/caruana-hanstock-bournemouth.doc.

Case, Peter and Selvester, Ken (2000), 'Close encounters: ideological invasion and complicity on an international management master's programme'. *Management Learning*, 31(1): 11–23.

— (2002), 'Watch your back: reflections on trust and mistrust in management education'. *Management Learning*, 33(2): 231–42.

Cassidy, Simon and Eachus, Peter (2000), 'Learning style, academic belief systems, self-report student proficiency and academic achievement in higher education'. *Educational Psychology*, 20(3): 307–22.

Causey, V., Thomas, C. and Armento, B. (1999), 'Cultural diversity is basically a foreign term to me: the challengers of diversity for pre-service teacher education'. *Teaching and Teacher Education*, 16(6): 33–45.

Chaabane, A.S and Mouss, L.H. (1998), 'The north-south dialogue through higher education'. *Higher Education Policy*, 11: 81–93.

Chalmers, D. and Volet, S. (1997), 'Common misconceptions about students from S.E. Asia studying in Australia'. *Higher Education Research and Development*, 16: 87–98.

Chan, C., Tsui, M.S., Chan, Y.C. and Hong, J.H. (2002), 'Applying the Structure of the Observed Learning Outcomes (SOLO) taxonomy on students' learning outcomes: an empirical study'. *Assesssment and Evaluation in Higher Education*, 27(6): 511–27.

Chan, S. (1999), 'The Chinese learner – a question of style'. *Education and Training*, 41: 6–7.

Chan, Wendy, W.Y. (2004), 'International cooperation in higher education: theory and practice'. *Journal of Studies in International Education*, 8(1): 32–55.

Chang, M.J. and Astin, A.W. (1997) 'Who benefits from racial diversity in higher eduation?' *Diversity Digest*, 1(2), 13, 16.

Chanock, K. (2004), *Introducing Students to the Culture of Enquiry in an Arts Degree*. New South Wales. Higher Education Research and Development Society of Australasia. Milperra.

Chapman, Anne and Pyvis, David (2005), 'Identity and social practice in higher education: student experiences of postgraduate courses delivered "Offshore" in Singapore and Hong Kong by an Australian university'. *International Journal of Educational Development*, 25: 39–52.

Cheng, X. (2000), 'Asian students' reticence revisited'. *System*, 28: 435–46.

Churchman, Deborah (2006), 'Institutional commitments, individual compromises: identity-related responses to compromise in an Australian university'. *Journal of Higher Education Policy and Management*, 28(1): 3–15.

Ciges, Auxiliadora Sales (2001), 'Online learning: new educational environments in order to respect cultural diversity through cooperative strategies'. *Intercultural Education*, 12(2): 135–47.

Clark, Burton R. (1997), 'Common problems and adaptive responses in the universities of the world: organizing for change'. *Higher Education Policy*, 103/4: 291–95.

Clark, H. and Brennan, S. (1991) 'Grounding in communication' in L.B. Resnick, J.M. Levine and S.D. Teasley (eds) *Perspectives on Socially Shared Cognition* (pp. 127–149) Washington D.C.: American Psychology Association.

Claxton, G. (1996a), 'Implicit theories of learning', in Claxton, G. and Atkinson, T. (eds), *Liberating the Learner: Lessons for Professional Development in Education*. London: Routledge, 45–58.

— (1996b), 'Integrated learning theory and the learning teacher', in Claxton, G. and Atkinson, T. (eds), *Liberating the Learner: Lessons for Professional Development in Education*. London: Routledge, 3–15.

Clayton, Thomas (2004), '"Competing Conceptions of Globalization" revisited: relocating the tension between world-systems analysis and globalization analysis'. *Comparative Education Review*, 48(3): 274–94.

Clyne, F. and Rizvi, F. (1998), 'Outcomes of student exchange', in Davis, D. and Olsen, A. (eds), *Outcomes of International Education*. Sydney: IDP *Education Australia*, 35–49.

Cortazzi, M. and Jin, L. (1996), 'Cultures of learning: language classrooms in China', in Coleman, H. (ed.), *Society and the Language Classroom*. Cambridge: Cambridge University Press, 169–206.

— (1997), 'Communication for learning across cultures', in McNamara, David and Harris, Robert (eds), *Overseas Students in Higher Education: Issues in Teaching and Learning*. London: Routledge, 76–90.

— (2001), 'Large classes in China: "good" teachers and interaction', in Watkins, D. and Biggs, J. (eds), *Teaching the Chinese Learner, Psychological and Pedagogical Perspectives*. Hong Kong: CERC/ACER, 115–34.

Crabtree, Robbin D. and Sapp, David Alan (2004), 'Your culture, my classroom, whose pedagogy? Negotiating effective teaching and learning in Brazil'. *Journal of Studies in International Education*, 8(1): 105–32.

Cranton, Patricia and Caruscetta, Ellen (2002), 'Reflecting on teaching: the influence of context'. *International Journal for Academic Development*, 7(2): 167–76.

Cruickshank, K. (2004), 'Towards diversity in teacher education: teacher preparation of immigrant teachers'. *European Journal of Teacher Education*. 27(2) June: 125–38.

Cushner, K. and Karim, A. (in press), 'Study abroad at the university level', in Landis, D. and Bennett, P. (eds), *Handbook of*

Intercultural Training (3rd edn). Thousand Oaks, CA: Sage.

Daly, A.J. and Barker, M.C. (2005), 'Australian and New Zealand university students' participation in international exchange programs'. *Journal of Studies in International Education*, 9: 26. jsi.sagepub.com/cgi/content/abstract/9/1/26.

De Jong, Huib and Teekens, Hanneke (2003), 'The case of university of Twente: internationalisation as education policy'. *Journal of Studies in International Education*, 7(1): 41–51.

De Vita, G. (2000), 'Inclusive approaches to effective communication and active participation in the multicultural classroom'. *Active Learning in Higher Education*, 1(2): 168–79.

— (2001), 'Learning styles, culture and inclusive instruction in the multicultural classroom: a business and management perspective'. *Innovations in Education and Teaching International*, 38(2): 165–74.

— (2002), 'Cultural equivalence in the assessment of home and international business management students: a UK exploratory study'. *Studies in Higher Education*, 27(2) 221–31.

— (2004), 'Integration and independent learning in a business synoptic module for international credit entry students'. *Teaching in Higher Education*, 9 (1): 69–81.

De Vita, Glauca and Case, Peter (2003), 'Rethinking the internationalisation agenda in UK higher education'. *Journal of Further and Higher Education*, 27(4): 383–98.

deWit, H. (ed) (1995), *Strategies for Internationalisation of Higher Education: A Comparative Study of Australia, Canada, Europe and the United States of America*. Amsterdam: EAIE.

— (2002), *Internationalization of Higher Education in the United States of America and Europe: A Historical, Comparative and Conceptual Analysis*. London: Greenwood Press.

Deardorff, Darla, K. (2006), 'Identification and assessment of intercultural competence as a student outcome of internationalization'. *Journal of Studies in International Education*, 110(3): 241–66.

Dearlove, John (1998), 'The deadly dull issue of university "administration"? Good governance, managerialism and organising academic work'. *Higher Education Policy*, 11: 59–79.

Deem, Rosemary (2001), 'Globalisation, new managerialism, academic capitalism and entrepreneurialism in universities: Is the local dimension still important?' *Comparative Education Review*, 37(1): 7–20.

Department for Education and Skills (DfES) (2006), *The UK Welcomes International Students*. www.dfes.gov.uk/international-students/tukwis.shtml.

Devos, Anita (2003), 'Academic standards, internationalization and the discursive construction of "the international student"'. *Higher Education Research and Development*, 22(2): 155–91.

Dixon, Mary (2006), 'Globalisation and international higher education: contested positionings'. *Journal of Studies in International Education*, 10(4): 319–33.

Dooley, Karen (2004), 'Pedagogy in diverse secondary school classes: legacies for higher education'. *Higher Education*, 48: 231–52.

Doorbar, Allison (2004), 'British Council trans-national education: qualitative market research findings'. Paper to Going Global Conference, Edinburgh.

Duke, Chris (2002), 'Cyperbole, commerce and internationalisation: "Desperate Hope and Desperate Fear"'. *Journal of Studies in International Education*, 6(2): 93–114.

Economist, The (2003a), 'Chinese students: western promise', 29 March–4 April: 33.

— (2003b), 'Education in China: a private matter', 29 March–4 April: 65–6.

Education Guardian (2005), 'We are in danger of driving international students away', 24 May. education.guardian.co.uk/higher/news/story/0,,1491187,00.html.

— (2006), 'The global challenge: an offer you can't refuse'. 5 May: 1.

Edwards, Richard and Usher, Robin (1997),'Final frontiers? Globalisation, pedagogy and (dis)location'. *Curriculum Studies*, 5(3): 253–67.

Edwards, Ron, Crosling, Glenda, Petrovic-Lazarovic S. and O'Neill, Peter (2003), 'Internationalization of business education: meaning and implementation'. *Higher Education Research and Development*, 22(2): 184–92.

Egege, Sandra and Kutieleh, Salah (2003), 'Critical thinking: teaching foreign notions to foreign students'. *International Education Journal*, 4(4): 75–85.

Ellingboe, B.J. (1998). 'Divisional strategies to internationalize a campus portrait: Results, resistance, and recommendations from a case study at a U.S. university', in Mestenhauser, J.A. and Ellingboe, B.J. (eds), *Reforming the Higher Education Curriculum: Internationalizing the Campus*. Phoenix, AZ: Oryx Press, 198–228.

Enders, Jurgen (2004), 'Higher education, internationalization and the nation-state: recent development and challenges to governance theory'. *Higher Education*, 47: 361–82

Ennis, R.H. (1985), 'A logical basis for measuring critical thinking skills'. *Educational Leadership*, 43(2): 44–8.

Ensor, Paula (2004), 'Contesting discourses in higher education: curriculum restructuring in South Africa'. *Higher Education*, 48(3): 339–59.

Erlenawati, S. (2005), 'Language difficulties of international students in Australia: the effects of prior learning experience'. *International Education Journal*, 6(5).

Errey, L. (2002), 'Plagiarism. something fishy . . . or just a fish out of water?' *Teaching Forum*, 50: 17–20.

Errington, E. (2004), 'The impact of teacher beliefs on flexible learning innovation: some practices and possibilities for academic developers'. *Innovations in Education and Teaching International*, 41(1): 39–47.

Europa Education and Training (2007), 'The Bologna process: towards the European higher education area'. ec.europa.eu/education/policies/educ/bologna/bologna_en.html.

Facione, P. A. (1990). *The Delphi Report*. Millbrae, CA: California Academic Press.

Fantini, A. E., Arias-Galicia, F. and Guay, D. (2001), 'Globalization and 21st century competencies: challenges for North American higher education'. Working Paper No. 11, Consortium for North American Higher Education Collaboration. conahec.org.

Farquhar, Robin, H. (1999), 'Integration or isolation: internationalism and the internet in Canadian higher education'. *Journal of Higher Education Policy and Management*, 21(1): 5–15.

Feast, Vicki and Bretag, Tracey (2005), 'Responding to rises in transnational education: new challenges for higher education'. *Higher Education Research and Development*, 24(1): 63–78.

Flowerdew, J. and Miller, L. (1995), 'On the notion of culture in L2 lectures'. *TESOL Quarterly*, 29(2): 345–73.

Forbes, Linda and Hamilton, John (2004), 'Building an international student market: educational-balanced scorecard solutions for regional Australian cities'. *International Education Journal*, 5(4): 502–20.

Fraser, K. (2001), 'Australian academic developers' conceptions of the profession'. *International Journal for Academic Development*, 6: 54–64.

Fraser, S.P. (2006), 'Shaping the university curriculum through partnerships and critical conversations'. *International Journal for Academic Development*, 11(1): 5–17.

Gabb, Diane (2006), 'Transcultural dynamics in the classroom'. *Journal of Studies in International Education*, 10(4): 357–68.

Gacel-Avila, Jocelyne (2005), 'The internationalisation of higher education: a paradigm for global citizenry'. *Journal of Studies in International Education*, 9(2): 121–36.

Gallego, M.A., and Hollingsworth, S. (eds) (2000), *What Counts as Literacy: Challenging School Standards*. New York: Teachers College, Columbia University.

Gardner, H. (1983), *Frames of Mind: The Theory of Multiple Intelligences*. New York: Basic Books.

Gatfield, T.J. (1997), 'International marketing of Australian higher education to Asia: a comparative study of Australian and Asian student perceptions of quality and its implications for the praxis of educators, policy makers and marketing practitioners'. Unpublished doctoral dissertation, Brisbane: Griffith University.

Gatfield, Terry, Barker, Michelle and Graham, Peter (1999), 'Measuring student quality variables and the implications for management practices in higher education institutions: an Australian and international student perspective'. *Journal of Higher Education Policy and Management*, 21(2): 239–52.

Gelter, H. (2003), 'Why is reflective thinking uncommon?' *Reflective Practice*, 4(3): 337–44.

Gibbs, Paul (2001), 'Higher education as a market: a problem or solution?' *Studies in Higher Education*, 26: 85–94.

Gibbons, Michael (1998), 'A commonwealth perspective on the globalization of higher education', in Scott, Peter (ed.), *The Globalization of Higher Education*. Buckingham: Open University Press, 70–87.

Gibbs, G., Habeshaw, T. and Yorke, M. (2000), 'Institutional learning and teaching strategies in English higher education'. *Higher Education*, 40: 351–72.

Gibbs, G. and Simpson, C. (2004), 'Conditions under which assessment supports students' learning'. *Learning and Teaching in Higher Education*, 1: 3–31.

Gil, M.C., and Katsara, R. (1999), 'The experiences of Spanish and Greek students in adapting to UK higher education: the creation of new support strategies'. Paper presented at British Educational Research Association Annual Conference, University of Sussex, Brighton. www.leeds.ac.uk/educol/documents/00001725.htm.

Gilbert, R. (2005), 'Social education and curriculum form: issues in selecting and articulating curriculum'. Paper presented to the Annual Conference of the Australian Association for Research in Education, Sydney, November.

Gillespie, Susan, H. (2002), 'The practice of international education in the context of globalization: a critique'. *Journal of Studies in International Education*, 6(3): 262–7.

Ginns, G. (1995), 'Research into student learning', in Smith, B. and Brown, S. (eds), *Research, Teaching and Learning in Higher Education*. London: Kogan Page, 19–29.

Golz, Reinhard (2005), 'Introduction: educational transformations without the consideration of international experiences seldom last', in Golz, Reinhard (ed.), *Internationalization, Cultural Difference and Migration: Challenges and Perspectives of Intercultural Education*. London: Transaction Publishers, 7–10.

Gosling, David (2003), 'Philosophical approaches to academic development' in Eggins, Heather and McDonald, Ranald (eds), *The Scholarship of Academic Development*. Buckingham: Open University Press, 70–9.

Gourlay, L. (2006), 'Negotiating boundaries: student perceptions, academic integrity and the co-construction of academic literacies'. Second International Plagiarism Conference, The Sage, Gateshead, 19-21 June. Newcastle: Northumbria University Press. www.jiscpas.ac.uk/2006papers.php.

Green. A. (1997), *Education, Globalization and the Nation State*. London: Macmillan.

Green M.F. (2003), 'The challenge of internationalizing undergraduate education: global learning for all'. Global Challenges and US Higher Education Conference, Duke University, Durham, NC. www.jhfc.duke.edu/ducis/globalchallenges/pdf/green.pdf.

Green, M.F. and Olsen, C.L. (2003), *Internationalizing the Campus: A User's Guide*. American Council on Education, Center for Institutional and International Initiatives, Washington, DC.

Gregory, E. and Williams, A. (2000), *City Literacies: Learning to Read Across Generations and Cultures*. London and New York: Routledge.

Halstead, J. Mark (2004), 'An Islamic concept of education'. *Comparative Education*, 40(4).

Hamilton, David (1999), 'The pedagogic paradox (or why no didactics in England?)' *Pedagogy, Culture and Society*, 7(1): 135–52.

Hanassab, Shideh (2006), 'Diversity, international students and perceived discrimination: implications for educators and counselors'. *Journal of Studies in International Education*, 10(2): 157–72.

Hanassab, Shideh and Tidwell, Romeria (2002), 'International students in higher education: identification of needs and implications for policy and practice'. *Journal of Studies in International Education*, 6(4): 305–22.

Hanna, Donald E. and Latchem, Colin (2002), 'Beyond national borders: transforming higher education institutions'. *Journal of Studies in International Education,* 6(2): 115–33.

Harland, Tony and Staniforth, David (2003), 'Academic development as academic work'. *International Journal for Academic Development,* 8(1/2): 25–35.

Harman, G. (2003), 'International Ph.D. students in Australian universities: financial support, course experience and career plans'. *International Journal of Educational Development,* 23: 339–51.

Harris, V. (2003), 'Adapting classroom-based strategy instruction to a distance learning context'. *TESL-EJ,* 7(2):1–16.

Hatakenaka, Sachi (2004), *Internationalism in Higher Education: a Review.* Higher Education Policy Institute. www.hepi.ac.uk/pubs. asp?DOC=Reports.

HEA (2007), 'What is learned at university: the social and organizational mediation of university learning (SOMUL) project'. www.open.ac.uk/cheri/pdfs/somul_wp04.pdf.

Healey, Mick and Jenkins, Alan (2003), 'Discipline-based educational development' in Eggins, Heather and McDonald, Ranald (eds), *The Scholarship of Academic Development.* Buckingham: Open University Press, 47–57.

Held, D., McGrew, A., Goldblatt, D. and Perraton, J. (1999), *Global Transformations: Politics, Economics and Culture.* Stanford, CA: Stanford University Press.

Hellsten, M. (2002), 'Students in transition: needs and experience of international students in Australia'. Paper presented at the 16th Australian International Education Conference, Hobart, Tasmania.

Hellsten, Meeri and Prescott, Anne (2004), 'Learning at university: the international student experience'. *International Education Journal,* 5(3): 344–51.

Henderson, M.W. (1996), 'Support provision in higher educational institutions for non UK postgraduate students'. *Journal for Further and Higher Education in Scotland,* 20(1): 18–22.

Henkel, M. (2000), *Academic Identities and Policy Change in Higher Education.* London: Jessica Kingsley.

HEPI (Higher Education Policy Institute) (2006), 'How exposed are English universities to reductions in demand from international students?' www.hepi.ac.uk/pubs.asp?DOC=Reports.

Heyneman, Stephen, P. (2001), 'The growing international commercial market for educational goods and services'. *International Journal of Educational Development,* 21: 345–59.

Higher Education Funding Council (HEFC) (2004), 'Effective practice with e-learning. www.jisc.ac.uk.

— (2006), 'Innovative practice with e-learning'. www.jisc.ac.uk/

uploaded_documents/InnovativePE.pdf.

Hill, Jeanne, Puurula, Arja, Sitko-Lutek, Agnieszka and Rakowska, Anna (2000), 'Cognitive style and socialisation: an exploration of learned sources of style in Finland, Poland and the UK'. *Educational Psychology*, 20(3): 285–305.

Hills, Steve and Thom, Viv (2005), 'Crossing a multicultural divide: teaching business strategy to students from culturally mixed backgrounds'. *Journal of Studies in International Education*, 9(4): 316–36.

Ho, A., Watkins, D. and Kelly, M. (2001), 'The conceptual change approach to improving teaching and learning: an evaluation of a Hong Kong staff development programme'. *Higher Education*, 42: 143–69.

Hodges, Lucy (2001), 'A cultural revolution for the 21st Century'. *The Independent*, 31 May.

Hoffman D.M. (2003), 'Internationalisation at home from the inside: non-native faculty and transformation'. *Journal of Studies in International Education*, 7(1): 77–93.

Hofstede, Geert (1984), *Culture's Consequences: International Differences in Work-Related Values*. London: Sage.

Holmes, P. (2004), 'Negotiating differences in learning and intercultural communication'. *Business Communication Quarterly*, 67(3): 294–307.

Huang Jianyi (1997), *Chinese Students and Scholars in American Higher Education*. London: Praeger.

Huczynski, A. and Buchanan, D. (2001), 'Learning', in *Organizational Behaviour: An Introductory Text* (4th edn), Chapter 4. Harlow: Prentice Hall, 107–27.

Hufton, Neil R., Elliott, Julian G. and Illushin, Leonid (2002), 'Educational motivations and engagement: qualitative accounts from three countries'. *British Educational Research Journal*, 28(2): 265–89.

Hui, Leng (2005), 'Chinese cultural schema of education: implications for communication between Chinese students and Australian educators'. *Issues in Educational Research*, 15(1): 17–36.

Humfrey, Christine (1999), *Managing International Students*. Buckingham: Open University Press.

Hyland, F. (2001), 'Dealing with plagiarism when giving feedback'. *English Language Teaching Journal*, 55(4): 375–81.

IDP Education Australia (1995), *Curriculum Development for Internationalisation. Australian Case Studies and Stocktake*. Canberra: Australian Government Publishing Service.

— (2003), 'International students in Australian universities'. //

www.idp.com/marketingandresearch/research/international educationstatistics/article411.asp.

IDP Education Australia (2007), 'International students in Australia'. www.idp.com/research/fastfacts/article406.asp.

IDP Education Australia and Australian Education International (2001), *Comparative Costs of Higher Education Courses for International Students in Australia, New Zealand, the United Kingdom, Canada and the United States.* Sydney: IDP Education Australia and AEI.

Illeris, K. (2002), *The Three Dimensions of Learning. Contemporary Learning Theory in the Tension Field between the Cognitive, the Emotional and the Social.* Frederiksberg: Roskilde University Press / Leicester, NIACE Publications.

Industry Task Force on Leadership and Management Skills (1995), *Enterprising Nation: Renewing Australia's Managers to Meet the Challenges of the Asia-Pacific Century.* Canberra: Australian Government Publishing Service.

Introna, L. and Hayes, N. (2004), 'Plagiarism, detection and intentionality: on the construction of plagiarists'. Plagiarism: Prevention, Practice and Policy Conference, St James Park, Newcastle upon Tyne, 28–30 June. Newcastle: Northumbria University Press, pp.-83–95 www.jiscpas.ac.uk/2004papers.php.

Ivy, Jonathan and Naudé, Peter (2004), 'Succeeding in the MBA marketplace: identifying the underlying factors'. *Journal of Higher Education Policy and Management,* 26(3): 401–17.

Jary, D. (2002), 'Benchmarking and quality management – the debate in UK higher education'. Birmingham: C-SAP Association for Lecturers in EAP.

Jeog-eun Rhee and Sagaria, M.A.D. (2004), 'International students: constructions of imperialism'. *Review of higher Education,* 28 (1): 77–96.

Jin, L. and Cortazzi, M. (2002), 'Cultural synergy: using Chinese strengths for learning in EAP'. British Association for Lecturers in EAP. www.baleap.org.uk/.

Johnson, K. and Inoue, Y. (2003), 'Diversity and multiculturalism'. *Journal of Research in International Education,* 2(3): 251–76.

Johnson, Rachel N. and Deem, Rosemary (2003), 'Talking of students: tensions and contradictions for the manager academic and the university in contemporary higher education'. *Higher Education,* 46: 289–314.

Jones, A. (2005), 'Culture and context: critical thinking and student learning in introductory macroeconomics'. *Studies in Higher Education,* 30(3): 339–54.

Jones, P.C. and Merritt, J.Q. (1999), 'The TALESSI Project: promoting active learning for interdisciplinarity, values awareness and critical thinking in environmental higher education'. *Journal of Geography in Higher Education*, 23(3): 335–48.

Kawaguchi, Akiyoshi and Lander, Dennis (1997), 'Internationalization in practice in Japanese universities'. *Higher Education Policy*, 10(2): 103–10.

Kelly, P. (1999), 'Internationalization of the curriculum'. Cited in *Achieving Diversity and Inclusivity in Teaching and Learning at the University of Western Australia*. Centre for Staff Development: University of Western Australia. www.osds.uwa.au.

Kember, D. (2000), 'Misconceptions about the learning approaches, motivation and study practices of Asian students'. *Higher Education*, 40(1): 99–121.

Kempner, Ken and Makino, Misao (1993), 'Cultural influences on construction of knowledge in Japanese higher education'. *Comparative Education*, 29(2): 185–99.

Kim Hye-Kyung (2003), 'Critical thinking, learning and Confucius: a positive assessment'. *Journal of Philosophy of Education*, 37: 71–87.

Kingston, E. and Forland, H. (2004), 'Bridging the gap in expectations between international students and academic staff – "At home the teachers feed me knowledge, but in the UK they help me to pick up the spoon and learn to feed myself!"' www.leeds.ac.uk/educol/documents/00003751.htm.

Kishun, Roshen (1998), 'Internationalization in South Africa', in Scott, Peter (ed.), *The Globalization of Higher Education*. Buckingham: Open University Press, 58–69.

Knight, J. (1999), *Internationalisation of Higher Education in IMHE Quality and Internationalisation in Higher Education*. Paris: OECD.

— (2000), *Progress and Promise: the AUCC Report on Internationalization at Canadian Universities*. Ottawa: Association of Universities and Colleges of Canada.

— (2001), 'Monitoring the quality and progress of internationalization'. *Journal of Studies in International Education*: 228–43.

— (2003), 'Updated internationalization definition'. *International Higher Education*, 33: 2–3.

— (2004), 'Internationalization remodelled: definition, approaches and rationales'. *Journal of Studies in International Education*, 8(1): 5–31.

Knight, Peter T. (2002), *Being a Teacher in Higher Education*.

Buckingham: Open University Press.

Kogan, M. (2000), 'Higher education communities and academic identity', in McNay, I. (ed.), *Higher Education and its Communities*. Buckingham: Open University Press.

— (2005), 'Modes of knowledge and power'. *Higher Education*, 49: 9–30.

Kolb, D. A. (1984), 'The Process of experimental learning' in Kolb, D., *The Experiential Learning: Experience as the Source of Learning and Development*. New York: Prentice-Hall.

Kumar, Rajesh and Usunier, Jean-Claude (2001), 'Management Education in a Globalizing World'. *Management Learning*, 32(3): 363–91.

Lambrech, Régine (1998), 'Quality management in the midst of chaos: the case for strategic management in the international office'. *Quality in Higher Education*, 4(1): 163–72.

Land, Ray (2001), 'Agency, context and change in academic development'. *The International Journal for Academic Development*, 6(1): 4–20.

Leask, B. (1999), 'Internationalisation of the curriculum: key challenges and strategies'. Invited paper presented at The State of the Art in Internationalising the Curriculum: International Perspectives, Australian International Education Conference, 5 October 1999. Australia: IDP Education. www.unisanet.unisa. edu.au/learningconnection/staff/practice/internationalisation/ documents/InternationalisationCurriculumPerth.pdf.

— (2000), 'Internationalisation: Changing contexts and their implications for teaching, learning and assessment'. HERDSA conference, available at www.aset.org.au/confs/aset-herdsa2000/ procs/leask1.htm.

— (2001), 'Bridging the gap: internationalising university curricula'. *Journal of Studies in International Education*, 5(2): 100–15.

— (2005), 'Internationalisation of the curriculum: teaching and learning', in Carroll, Jude and Ryan, Janette (eds), *Teaching International Students: Improving Learning for All*. London: Routledge, 119–29.

Leonard, D. and Morley, L. (2003), *The Experiences of International Students in UK Higher Education: a Review of Unpublished Research*. London: Institute of Education, University of London.

Le Roux, Johann (2001), 'Social dynamics of the multicultural classroom'. *Intercultural Education*, 12(3): 273–88.

— (2002), 'Effective educators are culturally competent communicators'. *Intercultural Education*, 13(1): 37–48.

Leung, Frederick, K.S. (2001), 'In search of an East Asian identity in mathematics education'. *Educational Studies in Mathematics*, 47(1): 35–51.

Lewis, Lionel L. and Altbach, Philip G. (1996), 'Faculty versus administration: a universal problem'. *Higher Education Policy*, 9(3): 255–8.

Liddicoat, A. (2004), 'Internationalisation as education'. Paper presented at seminar on The Intercultural in teaching and Learning, University of South Australia, 21 June.

Light, Gregory (2003), 'Realizing academic development: a model for embedding research practice in the practice of teaching', in Eggins, Heather and McDonald, Ranald (eds), *The Scholarship of Academic Development*. Buckingham: Open University Press, 152–64.

Lillis, R. (2006), 'What is an "academic literacies" approach to student writing and how might it inform our thinking about pedagogy, assessment practice and curriculum design?' Workshop delivered at Glasgow University, February.

Lillis, T. and Turner, J. (2001), 'Student writing in higher education: contemporary confusion, traditional concerns'. *Teaching in Higher Education*, 6(1): 58–68.

Lindahl, Ronald (2006), 'The right to education in a globalized world'. *Journal of Studies in International Education*, 10(1): 5–26.

Lipman, M. (2003), *Thinking in Education* (2nd edn). Cambridge: Cambridge University Press.

Liston, Colleen (2004), 'Issues and risks of offshore programs'. Paper to Going Global Conference, Edinburgh, December.

Littlemore, J. (2001), 'The use of metaphor in university lectures and the problems that it causes for overseas students'. *Teaching in Higher Education*, 6(3): 333–49.

Littlewood, W.T. and Liu, N.F. (1996), *Hong Kong Students and their English*. Hong Kong: Macmillan.

—-(1999), 'Defining and developing autonomy in East Asian contexts'. *Applied Linguistics*, 20(1),:71–94.

Liu, N.F. and Littlewood, W. (1997), 'Why do many students appear reluctant to participate in classroom learning discourse?' *System*, 25(3): 371–84.

Livingstone, K., Soden, R. and Kirkwood, M. (2004), *Post-16 Pedagogy and Thinking Skills; an Evaluation*. London: Learning and Skills Research Centre.

Lord, P.A. and Dawson, C. (2003), 'The induction needs of international students at postgraduate level, faculty of professional studies, Thames Valley University'. www.businesss.heacademy. ac.uk/resources/reflect/conf/2003/lord/lord.pdf.

Luijten-Lub, Anneke, Van der Wende, Marijk and Huisman, Jeroen (2005), 'On cooperation and competition'. *Journal of Studies in International Education*, 9(2): 147–63.

Luzio-Lockett, A. (1998), 'The squeezing effect: the cross-cultural experience of international students'. *British Journal of Guidance and Counselling*, 26(2): 209–23.

Maassen, P. (1996), *Governmental Steering and the Academic Culture: The Intangibility of the Human Factor in Dutch and German Universities.* Maarsen: De Tijdstroom.

McAlpine, Lynn (2006), 'Coming of age in a time of super-complexity (with apologies to both Mead and Barnett)'. *International Journal for Academic Development*, 11(2): 123–7.

McDonald, Ranald (2003), 'Developing the scholarship of academic development: setting the context', in Eggins, Heather and McDonald, Ranald (eds), *The Scholarship of Academic Development.* Buckingham: Open University Press, 1–12.

McKenzie, Aileen, Bourn, Douglas, Evans, Simon, Brown, Maidi, Shiel, Chris, Bunney, Andrew, Collins, Gwen, Wade, Ros, Parker, Jenneth and Annette, John (2003), *Global Perspectives in Higher Education.* Development Education Association. www.dea.org.uk/publication-49dce788dc041c29d9046352de814a5.

Mackinnon, D. and Manathunga, C. (2003), 'Going global with assessment: what to do when the dominant culture's literacy drives assessment'. *Higher Education Research and Development*, 22(2): 131–44.

Mackinnon, Valerie. J. (1998), 'Exporting professional courses: cultural and educational implications'. *Higher Education Policy*, 11: 311–22.

McNamara, David and Harris, Robert (eds) (1997), *Overseas Students in Higher Education: Issues in Teaching and Learning.* London: Routledge.

Macrae, Murray (1997), 'The induction of international students to academic life in the United Kingdom', in McNamara, David and Harris, Robert (eds), *Overseas Students in Higher Education: Issues in Teaching and Learning.* London: Routledge, 127–42.

McTaggart, R. (2003), 'Internationalisation of the curriculum: a discussion paper'. www.jcu.edu.au/office/tld/teachingsupport/documents/International_Curriculum-AB.pdf.

McWilliam, Erica, Hatcher, Caroline and Meadmore, Daphne (1999), 'Developing professional identities: remaking the academic for corporate times'. *Pedagogy, Culture and Society*, 7:1, 55–72.

Magolda, M.B. (1992), *Knowing and Reasoning in College: Gender-Related Patterns in Students' Intellectual Development.* San

Francisco: Jossey-Bass.

Major, Elza Magalhaes (2005), 'Co-national support, cultural therapy, and the adjustment of Asian students to an English-speaking university culture'. *International Education Journal*, 6(1): 84–95.

Mak, A.S., Westwood, M.J., Ishiyama, F.I. and Barker, M.C. (1999), 'Optimising conditions for learning sociocultural competencies for success'. *International Journal of Intercultural Relations*, 23 (1): 77–89.

Mallinckrodt, B. and Leong, F.T. (1992), 'Social support in academic programs and family environments: sex differences and role conflicts for graduate students'. *Journal of Counceling and Development*, 70: 716–24.

Malthus, C. and Gunn-Lewis, J. (2000), 'Dialogue with adult overseas students: reflections on experiences of teaching and learning'. *New Zealand Journal of Adult Learning*, 28(1): 50–67.

Manathunga, Catherine (2006), 'Doing educational development ambivalently: applying post-colonial metaphors to educational development?' *International Journal for Academic Development*, 11(1): 19–29.

Marginson, Simon (2000), 'Rethinking academic work in the global era'. *Journal of Higher Education Policy and Management*, 22(1): 23–35.

Marshall, J. and Martin, B. (2000), 'The boundaries of belief: territories of encounter between indigenous peoples and western philosophies'. *Educational Philosophy and Theory*, 32(1).

Martinsons, M.G. and Martinsons, A.B. (1996), 'Conquering cultural constraints to cultivate Chinese management creativity and innovation'. *Journal of Management Development*. 15(9): 18–35.

Marton, F. (1976), 'What does it take to learn? Some implications of an alternative view of learning', in Entwistle, N. (ed.), *Strategies for Research and Development in Higher Education*. Amsterdam: Swets & Zeitlinger, 32–42.

Marton, F. and Säljö, R. (1976), 'On qualitative differences in learning'. *British Journal of Educational Psychology*, 46:4–11.

Marton, Ference, Wen Qiufang and Wong, Kam Cheung (2005), '"Read a hundred times and the meaning will appear . . ." Changes in Chinese university students' views of the temporal structure of learning'. *Higher Education*, 49: 291–318.

Mason, J. and Stanley, D. (1997), *Preparing Graduates for the Future: International Learning Outcomes*. Victoria BC: Centre for International Education.

Matthews, Julie (2002), 'International education and internationalisation are not the same as globalisation: emerging issues for secondary schools'. *Journal of Studies in International Education*, 6(4): 369–90.

Mayor, Frederico (1998), 'The universal university'. *Higher Education Policy*, 11: 249–55.

Mazzarol, T. and Soutar, G.N. (2002), '"Push-pull" factors influencing international student destination choice'. *The International Journal of Educational Management*, 16(2): 82–90.

Meek, Lynn (2000), 'Diversity and marketization of higher education: incompatible concepts?' *Higher Education Policy*, 13: 23–39.

Meiras, Sandra (2004), 'International education in Australian universities: understandings, dimensions and problems'. *Journal of Higher Education Policy Management*, 26(3): 371–80.

Mestenhauser, J.A. (1998), 'Portraits of an international curriculum: an uncommon multidimensional perspective', in Mestenhauser, Josef A. and Ellingboe, Brenda J. (eds), *Reforming the Higher Education Curriculum: Internationalizing the Campus*. Phoenix, AZ: Oryx Press.

— (2000), 'Missing in action: leadership for international and global education for the twenty-first century', in Barrows, L.C. (ed.), *Internationalization of Higher Education: An Institutional Perspective. Papers on Higher Education*. United Nations Educational, Scientific, and Cultural Organization: Bucharest European Centre for Higher Education, 23–62.

MEXT (Ministry of Education, Culture, Sports, Science and Technology, Japan) (2004), *Outline of the Student Exchange System in Japan*.

Mezirow, J. (2000), 'Learning to think like an adult: core concepts of transformation theory', in Mezirow, J. (ed.), *Learning as Transformation: Critical Perspectives on a Theory in Progress*. San Francisco, CA: Jossey-Bass, 3–33.

Middlehurst, Robin and Woodfield, Steve (2006), 'Quality review in distance learning: policy and practice in five countries'. *Tertiary Education and Management*, 12(1): 37–58.

— (2007), *Research Project Report 05/06: Responding to the Internationalisation Agenda: Implications for Institutional Strategy*. Higher Education Academy. www.heacademy.ac.uk/4265.htm.

Milstein, T. (2005), 'Transformation abroad: sojourning and the perceived enhancement of self-efficacy'. *International Journal of Intercultural Relations*, 29: 217–38.

Ministry of Education (2002a), *Tertiary Education Statistics*. www.minedu.govt.nz.

— (2002b), *Export Education Update*. www.minedu.govt.nz.

Minnis, J.R. (1999), 'Is reflective practice compatible with Malay-Islamic values? Some thoughts on teacher education in Brunei Durassalam'. *Australian Journal of Education*, 43(2): 172–83.

Mok, Ida, Chik, P.Y., Ko, Tammy Kwan, Lo, M.L., Marton, Ference, Ng, Dorothy F.P, Pang, M.F., Runesson, U. and Szeto, L.H. (2001), 'Solving the paradox of the Chinese teacher?' in Biggs, John B., Watkins, David A. and Brabazon, Tara (eds), *Teaching the Chinese Learner: Psychological and Pedagogical Perspectives*. Hong Kong: Hong Kong University Press.

Mok, Ka-Ho (2005), 'Globalization and educational restructuring: university merging and changing governance in China'. *Higher Education*, 50: 57–88.

Molesworth, Mike and Scullion, Richard (2005), 'The impact of commercially promoted vocational degrees on the student experience'. *Journal of Higher Education Policy and Management*, 27(2): 209–25.

Moon, S.M. (2003), 'Personal talent', *High Ability Studies*, 14(1): 5–23.

Morey, Ann I. (2004), 'Globalization and the emergence of for-profit higher education'. *Higher Education*, 48: 131–50.

Morey, A.I. and Kitano, M. (1997), 'Multicultural course transformation in higher education – a broader truth', as cited in Bournemouth University, Centre for Academic Practice, Literature Reviews Internationalisation and Globalisation: An Introduction to the Basics. www.bournemouth.ac.uk/centre-for-academic-practice/researchthemes.html.

Morgan, G. and Cohen, P. (2006), 'Introduction to the special issue on globalisation: narratives of education and work'. *Journal of Education and Work*. 19(2): 105–07.

Morrison, Jo, Merrick, Beatrice, Higgs, Samantha and Le Metais, Joanna (2005), 'Researching the performance of international Students in the UK'. *Studies in Higher Education*, 30(3): 327–37.

Mortimer, Kathleen (1997), 'Recruiting overseas undergraduate students: are their information requirements being satisfied?' *Higher Education Quarterly*, 51(3): 225–38.

Moseley, D., Baumfield, V., Elliott, J., Gregson, M., Higgins, S., Lin, M., Miller, J., Newton, D. and Robson, S. (2004), *Thinking Skill Frameworks for post-16 Learners: an Evaluation*. London: Learning and Skills Research Council.

Moseley, D., Elliott, J., Gregson, M. and Higgins, S. (2005), 'Thinking skills frameworks for use in education and training'. *British Educational Research Journal* 31(3): 367–90.

Moses, I. (2003), 'The university – a permanent factor in the development and advancement of society: views from institutions of higher education and academic organizations'. *Higher Education in Europe,* 28(1): 87–92.

Mulligan, D. and Kirkpatrick, A. (2000), 'How much do they understand? Lectures, students and comprehension'. *Higher Education Research and Development,* 19(3): 311–35.

Murphy, Patricia and Ivinson, Gabrielle (2003), 'Pedagogy and cultural knowledge: a sociocultural perspective'. *Pedagogy, Culture and Society,* 11(1): 5–9.

Naidoo, Prem (2004), 'Offshore higher education provision in South Africa: does it offer more, different and/or better higher education?' Paper to Going Global Conference, Edinburgh, December.

Nainby, K. E., Warren, J. T. and Bollinger, C. (2003), 'Articulating contact in the classroom: towards a constitutive focus in critical pedagogy'. *Language and Intercultural Communication,* 3(3): 198–212.

New Zealand Vice Chancellors' Committee (2002), *Annual Report 2000.* www.nvcc.ac.nz/pubs/vcanrep_00.pdf.

Newman, Michael, Trenchs-Parera, Mireira, Pujol, Merce (2003), 'Core academic literacy principles versus culture-specific practices: a multi-case study of academic achievement'. *English for Specific Purposes,* 22: 45–71.

Newton, D.P. (2000), *Teaching for Understanding.* London: Falmer Press.

Newton, D.P. and Newton, L.D. (1997) *Supporting Students' Understanding: Teaching for Understanding in Higher Education.* Durham: Clear View Press.

Nilsson, B. (2000), 'Internationalizing the curriculum', in Crowther, P., Joris, M., Otten, M., Nilsson, B., Teekens, H. and Wachter, B. (eds), *Internationalisation at Home: A Position Paper.* Amsterdam: European Association for International Education, 2–7.

Norton, L., Richardson, J.T.E., Hartley, J., Newstead, S. and Mayes, J. (2005), 'Teachers' beliefs and intentions concerning teaching in higher education'. *Higher Education,* 50: 537–71.

Norton, L., Tilley, A., Newstead, S. and Franklyn-Stokes, A. (2001), 'The pressures of assessment in undergraduate courses and their effect on student behaviours'. *Assessment and Evaluation in Higher Education,* 26(3): 269–84.

Odgers, T. and Giroux, I. (2006), 'Internationalizing faculty: a phased approach to transforming curriculum design and instruction'. Paper presented at the York University Annual International Conference on Internationalizing Canada's Universities, 2–3 March, Toronto, Ontario.

Ogbonna, Emmanuel and Harris, Lloyd, C. (2004), 'Work intensification and emotional labour among UK university lecturers: an exploratory study'. *Organization Studies*, 27(7): 1185–203.

Ohmori, F. (2004a), *Japan's Policy Changes to Recognise Transnational Higher Education: Adaptation of the National System to Globalisation?* London: The Observatory on Borderless Higher Education Report.

— (2004b), 'Japan and transnational higher education'. *Center for International Higher Education Newsletter*, 37.

Okorocha, E. (1996), 'The international student experience: expectations and realities'. *Journal of Graduate Education*, 2(3): 80–4.

Olsen, C.L. and Kroeger, K.R. (2001), 'Global competency and intercultural sensitivity'. *Journal of Studies in International Education*, 5(2): 116–37.

Olsen, C.L., Green, M.F. and Hill, B.A. (2005), *Building a Strategic Framework for Comprehensive Internationalization*. Washington, DC: American Council on Education.

Ortiz, Jaime (2004), 'International business education in a global environment: a conceptual approach'. *International Education Journal*, 5(2): 255–65.

Otten, M. (2000), 'Impacts of cultural diversity at home', in Crowther, P., Joris, M., Otten, M., Nilsson, B., Teekens, H. and Wachter, B. (eds), *Internationalisation at Home: A Position Paper*. Amsterdam: European Association for International Education, 15–20.

— (2003), 'Intercultural learning and diversity in higher education'. *Journal of Studies in International Education*, 7(1): 12–26.

Ottewill, Roger and MacFarlane, Bruce (2003), 'The pedagogic challenges facing business and management lecturers working in UK higher education: assessing the evidence'. *International Journal for Management Education*, 3(3): 33–41.

Padilla, R., Trevino, J., Gonzalez, K. and Trevino, J. (1997), 'Developing local models of minority student success in college'. *Journal of College Student Development*, 38(2): 125–35.

Paige, R.M. (2003), 'The American case: the University of Minnesota'. *Journal of Studies of International Education*, 7(1): 52–63.

Paige, R.M., and Mestenhauser, J.A. (1999), 'Internationalizing educational administration'. *Educational Administration Quarterly*, 35(4): 500–17.

Park, C. (2003), 'In other people's words: plagiarism by university students – literature and lessons'. *Assessment and Evaluation in*

Higher Education, 28(5): 471–88.

Parmenter, Lynne (1999), 'Constructing national identity in a changing world: perspectives in Japanese education'. *British Journal of Sociology of Education*, 20(4): 453–63.

Pascarella E.T. and Terenzini, P.T. (2005), *How College Affects Students* (Vol 2): *A Third Decade of Research*. San Francisco: Jossey-Bass.

Paterson, Lindsay (2001), 'Higher education and European regionalism'. *Pedagogy, Culture and Society*, 9(2): 133–60.

Pecorari, D. (2003), 'Good and original: plagiarism and patchworking in academic second language writing'. *Journal of Second Language Writing*, 12: 317–45.

Pennycook, Alistair (1994), *The Cultural Politics of English as an International Language*. Harlow: Longman.

— (1996), 'Borrowing others' words: text, ownership, memory and plagiarism'. *TESOL Quarterly*, 30(2): 210–30.

— (1998), *English and the Discourses of Colonialism*. London: Routledge.

Peters, Michael (2004), 'Higher education, globalization and the knowledge economy', in Walker, Melanie and Nixon, John (eds) *Reclaiming Universities from a Runaway World*. Buckingham: Open University Press.

Pettigrew, T.F. and Tropp, L.R. (2000), 'Does intergroup contact reduce prejudice? Recent meta-analytic findings', in Oskamp, S. (ed.), *Reducing Prejudice and Discrimination. The Claremont Symposium on Applied Social Psychology*. Mahwah, NJ: Laurence Erlbaum Associates, 93–114.

Pintrich, P.R. (2000), 'The role of goal orientation in self-regulated learning', in Boekaerts, M., Pintrich, P.R. and Zeidner, M. (eds), *Handbook of Self-Regulation*. London: Academic Press.

Poole, David (2001), 'Moving towards professionalism: the strategic management of international education activities at Australian universities and their faculties of business'. *Higher Education*, 42: 395–435.

Postiglione, Gerard, A. (2005), 'China's global bridging: the transformation of university mobility between Hong Kong and the United States'. *Journal of Studies in International Education*, 91: 5–25.

Prime Minister's Initiative for International Education (2006), press notice, 'Prime Minister launches strategy to make UK leader in international education'. Department for Children, Schools and Families, 18 April. www.dfes.gov.uk/pns/DisplayPN.cgi?pn_id=2006_0058.

Pritchard, Rosalind M.O. and Skinner, Barbara (2002), 'Cross-cultural partnerships between home and international students'. *Journal of Studies in International Education*, 6(4): 323–54.

Radbourne, Jennifer (2006), 'A values approach to business education in Hong Kong'. *Industry and Higher Education*, 20(5): 307–15.

Ramburuth, Prem and McCormick, John (2001), 'Learning diversity in higher education: a comparative study of Asian international and Australian students'. *Higher Education*, 42(3): 333–50.

Rasool, Naz (2004), 'Exploring the construction of social class in educational discourse: the rational order of the nation state versus global uncertainties'. *Pedagogy, Culture and Society*, 12(1): 121–39.

Renzulli, J.S. and Reis, S.M. (1986), 'The three-ring conception of giftedness: a developmental model for creative productivity', in Sternberg, R.J. and Davidson, J.E. (eds), *Conceptions of Giftedness*. Cambridge: Cambridge University Press.

Reponen, Tapio (1999), 'Is leadership possible at loosely coupled organizations such as universities?' *Higher Education Policy*, 12: 237–44.

Richardson, J.T.E. and Edmunds, R. (2007), 'A cognitive developmental model of university learning'. Working paper on the Higher Education Academy project, What is learned at university: the social and organisational mediation of university learning, 4 February. York: Higher Education Academy (SOMUL). The Higher Education Academy and Open University/CHERI. www.open.ac.uk/cheri/pdfs/somul_wp04.pdf.

Richardson, P.M. (2004), 'Possible influences of Arabic-Islamic culture on the reflective practices proposed for an education degree at the Higher Colleges of Technology in the United Arab Emirates'. *International Journal of Educational Development*, 24: 429–36.

Ritchie, E. (2006) 'Internationalization: where are we going and how do we know when we have got there?' *Academy Exchange 5* (Winter): 13–15.

Rizvi, F. (2000), *Internationalisation of Curriculum*. Melbourne, RMIT University. www.pvci.rmit.edu.au/ioc/back/icpfr.pdf.

Rizvi, Fazal, Lingard, Bob and Lavia, Jennifer (2006), 'Postcolonialism and education: negotiating a contested terrain'. *Pedagogy, Culture and Society*, 14(3): 249–62.

Robertson, Margaret, Line, Martin, Jones, Susan and Thomas, Susan (2000), 'International students, learning environment and perceptions: a case study using the Delphi technique'. *Higher Education Research and Development*, 19(1): 89–102.

Robinson, V. and Kuin, L. (1999), 'The explanation of practice:

why Chinese students copy assignments'. *Qualitative Studies in Education*, 12(2): 193–210.

Robson, S. and Turner, Y. (2007), '"Teaching is a co-learning experience"; academics reflecting on learning and teaching in an "internationalised" faculty'. *Teaching in Higher Education*, 12(1): 41–54.

Rochford, Francine (2006), 'Is there *any* clear idea of a university?' *Journal of Higher Education Policy and Management*, 28(2): 147–58.

Rodwell, Susie (1998), 'Internationalisation or indigenisation of educational management development? Some issues of cross-cultural transfer'. *Comparative Education*, 34(1): 41–54.

Rorty, Richard (1980), *Philosophy and the Mirror of Nature*. Oxford: Blackwell.

Rouhani, Sepideh and Kishun, Roshen (2004), 'Introduction: internationalisation of higher education in (South) Africa'. *Journal of Studies in International Education*, 8(3): 235–43.

Rowland, S. (2001), 'Surface learning about teaching in higher education'. *International Journal for Academic Development*, 6(2): 62–167.

— (2002), 'Overcoming fragmentation in professional life: the challenge for academic development'. *Higher Education Quarterly*, 56(1): 52–64.

— (2003), 'Academic development: a practical or theoretical business?' in Eggins, Heather and McDonald, Ranald (eds), *The Scholarship of Academic Development*. Buckingham: Open University Press, 13–22.

Rowland, S., Byron, C., Furedi, F., Padfield, N. and Smyth, T. (1998), 'Turning academics into teachers?' *Teaching in Higher Education*, 3(2): 133–41.

Ryan, Janette (2000), *A Guide to Teaching International Students*. Oxford: Oxford Centre for Staff and Learning Development, Oxford Brookes University.

Säljö, R. (1979) 'Learning about learning'. *Higher Education*, 8: 443–51.

Samuelowicz, Katherine and Bain, John. D. (2001), 'Revisiting academics' beliefs about teaching and learning'. *Higher Education*, 41: 299–325.

Sanchez, I. (2000), 'Motivating and maximizing learning in minority classrooms', in Aragon, S. (ed.), *Beyond Access: Methods and Models for Increasing Retention and Learning among Minority Students*, San Francisco: Jossey-Bass, 35–44.

Sanderson, Gavin (2004), 'Existentialism, globalization and the cultural other'. *International Education Journal*, 4: 1–20.

Sastry, Tom (2004), *Postgraduate Education in the United Kingdom*, Higher Education Policy Institute, www.hepi.ac.uk/pubs. asp?DOC=Reports.

Scarino, A., Crichton, J. and Papademetre, L. (2005), 'A framework for quality assurance in the development and delivery of offshore programs in languages other than English'. Report prepared by the Research Centre for Languages and Cultures Education, in the School of International Studies at the University of South Australia for the Australian Vice Chancellors' Committee.

Schapper, Jan M. and Mayson, Susan E. (2004), 'Internationalisation of curricula: an alternative to the Taylorisation of academic Work'. *Journal of Higher Education Policy and Management*, 26(2): 189–205.

Schon, D.A. (1987), *Educating the Reflective Practitioner: Toward a New Design for Teaching and Learning in the Professions*. San Francisco, CA: Jossey-Bass.

Schroder, R.E.V.M. (2001), 'The international student in the classroom', in Teekens, H. (ed.), *Teaching and Learning in the International Classroom*. The Hague: NUFFIC, 48–56.

Scollon, R. (1995), 'Plagiarism and ideology: identity in intercultural discourse'. *Language and Society* 24(1): 1028.

Scott, Peter (1995), *The Meanings of Mass Higher Education*. Buckingham: Open University Press.

— (1998), 'Massification, internationalization and globalization', in Scott, Peter (ed.), *The Globalization of Higher Education*. Buckingham: Open University Press, 108–29.

Seelen, L.P. (2002), 'Is performance in English as a second language a relevant criterion for admission to an English medium university?' *Higher Education*, 44: 213–32.

Seo, Seonjin and Koro-Ljungberg, Mirka (2005), 'A hermeneutical study of older Korean graduate students' experiences in American higher education: from Confucianism to western educational values'. *Journal of Studies in International Education*, 9(2) 164–87.

Sharps, J. (1997), 'Communities of practice: a review of the literature'. www.tfriend.com/cop-lit.htm.

Shiel, C. (2006), 'Developing the global citizen higher education academy'. *Academy Exchange*, 5 (Winter).

Simon, Brian (1999), 'Why no pedagogy in England?' in Leach, Jenny and Moon, Bob (eds), *Learners and Pedagogy*. London: Sage, 34–45.

Singh, Basil, R. (2002), 'Problems and possibilities of dialogue across cultures'. *Intercultural Education*, 13(2): 215–27.

Singh, P. and Doherty, C. (2004), 'Global cultural flows and pedagogic dilemmas: teaching in the global university contact zone'. *TESOL Quarterly*, 38(1): 9–42.

Slaughter, S. and Leslie, G. (1997), *Academic Capitalism: Politics, Policies and the Entrepreneurial University*. Baltimore, MD: John S. Hopkins University Press.

Smith, Mark (1998), *Social Science in Question*. Buckingham: Open University Press.

Snyder, B. (1971), *The Hidden Curriculum*. New York: Alfred A. Knopf.

Soderqvist, M. (2002), *Internationalization and its Management at Higher-Education Institutions: Applying Conceptual, Content and Discourse Analysis*. Helsinki: Helsinki School of Economics.

Sowden, C. (2005), 'Plagiarism and the culture of multilingual students in higher education abroad'. *English Language Teaching, Journal* 59(3): 226–33.

Spencer-Oatey, H. and Xiong, Z. (2006), 'Chinese students' psychological and sociocultural adjustment to Britain: an empirical study'. *Language, Culture and Curriculum*, 19(1): 37–53.

Stefani, Lorraine and Matthew, Bob (2002), 'The difficulties of defining development: a case study'. *The International Journal for Academic Development*, 7(1): 41–50.

Stephens, K. (1997) 'Cultural stereotyping and intercultural communication: working with students from the People's Republic of China in the UK'. *Language and Education*, 11(2): 113–24.

Sternberg, R.J. (2003), *Wisdom, Intelligence, Creativity, Synthesized*. New York: Cambridge University Press.

Stier, J. (2002), 'Internationalisation in higher education: unexplored possibilities and unavoidable challenges'. European Conference on Educational Research, 11–14 September, Lisbon. www.leeds.ac.uk/educol/documents/00002342.htm.

— (2003), 'Internationalisation, ethnic diversity and the acquisition of intercultural competence'. *Intercultural Education*, 14(1).

Stoicovy, C. (2002), 'A case for culturally responsive pedagogy'. *International Research into Geographical and Environmental Education*, 11(1): 80–4.

Stone, Nick (2006), 'Conceptualising intercultural effectiveness for university teaching'. *Journal of Studies for International Education*, 10(4): 334–56.

Szalay, Leonard B., Strohl, Jean, Fu, Liu, Lao, Pen-Shui (1994), *American and Chinese Perceptions and Belief Systems: a People's Republic of China-Taiwanese Comparison*. New York: Plenum

Press.

Szekeres, Judy (2006), 'General staff experiences in the corporate university'. *Journal of Higher Education Policy and Management*, 28(2): 133–45.

Szelenyi, K. (2001), *Minority Student Retention and Academic Achievement in Community Colleges*. Los Angeles: ERIC clearing house for Community Colleges.

Tatar, Sibel (2005), 'Classroom participation by international students: the case of Turkish graduate students'. *Journal of Studies in International Education*, 9(4): 337–55.

Taylor, John (2002), 'Changes in teaching and learning in the period to 2005: the case of postgraduate higher education in the UK'. *Journal of Higher Education Policy and Management*, 24(1): 53–73.

— (2004), 'Toward a strategy for internationalisation: lessons and practice from four universities'. *Journal of Studies in International Education*, 8(2): 149–71.

Teekens, H. (2003), 'The requirement to develop specific skills for teaching in an intercultural setting'. *Journal of Studies in International Education*, 7(1): 108–19.

— (2005), 'Internationalization at home: a background paper'. International conference, 9–10 May, Rotterdam. www.nuffic.nl/ pdf/netwerk/Background-paper-iah.pdf.

Teichler, Ulrich (1996), 'The changing nature of higher education in western Europe'. *Higher Education Policy*, 9(2): 89–111.

— (1998), 'The role of the European Union in the internationalization of higher education', in Scott, Peter (ed.), *The Globalization of Higher Education*. Buckingham: Open University Press, 88–99.

— (1999), 'Higher education policy and the world of work: Changing conditions and challenges'. *Higher Education Policy*, 12: 285–312.

— (2004), 'The changing debate on internationalization of higher education'. *Higher Education*, 48: 5–26.

Teichler, U. and Jahr, V. (2001), 'Mobility during the course of study and after graduation'. *European Journal of Education*, 36(4): 443–58.

Terenzini, P. T., Springer, L., Yaeger, P., Pascarella, E. T. and Nora, A. (1996), 'First-generation college students: characteristics, experiences, and cognitive development'. *Research in Higher Education*, 37: 1–22.

Thomas, L. (2002), 'Student retention in higher education: the role of institutional habitus'. *Journal of Educational Policy*, 17(4): 423–42.

Thorstensson, Liv (2001), 'The business of internationalization: the academic experiences of 6 Asian MBA international students at the University of Minnesota's Carlson School of Management'. *Journal of Studies in International Education*, 5(4): 317–40.

Thune, Taran and Welle-Strand, Anne (2005), 'ICT for and in internationalization processes: a business school case study'. *Higher Education*, 50: 593–611.

Times Higher Education Supplement, The (2006a), 'Is the UK Starting to lose pulling power?' 22 December.

— (2006b), 'Foreign students put off by cost of living in the UK'. 2 November.

— (2006c), 'International cohort grows'. 15 September.

— (2006d), 'Overseas agent probe'. 1 December.

— (2007a), 'Nul points for our global tune'. 15 June.

— (2007b), 'Bologna means continental shift in UK'. 6 April

— (2007c), 'Linguistic challenge'. 12 January.

Tomlinson, B. and Dat, B. (2004), 'The contributions of Vietnamese learners of English to ELT methodology'. *Language Teaching Research*, 8(2): 199–222.

Tremblay, Karine (2005), 'Academic mobility and immigration'. *Journal of Studies in International Education*, 9(3): 196–228.

Trice, Andrea, G. (2005), 'Navigating in a multinational learning community: academic departments' responses to graduate international students'. *Journal of Studies in International Education*, 9(1): 62–89.

Trigwell, Keith (2003), 'A relational model approach for academic development', in Eggins, Heather and McDonald, Ranald (eds), *The Scholarship of Academic Development*. Buckingham: Open University Press, 23–33.

Trow, Martin (1996), 'Trust, markets and accountability in higher education: a comparative perspective'. *Higher Education Policy*, 9(4): 309–24.

Trowler, P. (1998), *Academics Responding to Change: New Higher Education Frameworks and Academic Cultures*. Buckingham: Open University Press/SRHE.

Trowler, P. and Cooper, A. (2002), 'Teaching and learning regimes: implicit theories and recurrent practices in the enhancement of teaching and learning through educational development programmes'. *Higher Education Research and Development*, 21(3): 221–40.

Trowler, P. and Knight, P. (2000), 'Coming to know in higher education: theorising faculty entry to new work contexts'. *Higher Education Research and Development*, 19(1): 27–42.

Tsui, A. (1996), 'Reticence and anxiety in second language learning', in Bailey, K. and Nunan, D. (eds), *Voices from the Language Classroom*. Cambridge, Cambridge University Press, 145–67.

Turner, Y. (2002a), 'Chinese students in Europe: the influence of culture and society', in Cox, W. and Cameron, D. (eds), *Chinese Students in Ireland: New Opportunities, New Needs, New Challenges*. Dublin: Irish Council for International Students.

— (2002b), 'When an unstoppable force meets an immovable object: Chinese students in UK universities', in Cox, W. and Cameron, D. (eds), *Chinese Students in Ireland: New Opportunities, New Needs, New Challenges*. Dublin: Irish Council for Overseas Students.

— (2006a), 'Chinese students in a UK business school: hearing the student voice in reflective teaching and learning practice'. *Higher Education Quarterly*, 60(1): 25–51.

— (2006b), 'Chinese students and critical thinking in postgraduate business and management degrees: teasing out tensions of culture, style and substance'. *International Journal of Management Education*, 5(1): 3–12.

Turner, Y. and Acker, A. (2002), *Education in the New China: Shaping Ideas at Work*. Basingstoke: Ashgate.

Turner, Y. and Robson, S. (2007), 'Competitive and cooperative impulses to internationalization: reflecting on the interplay between management intentions and the experience of academics in a British university'. *Education, Knowledge and Economy*, 1(1): 65–82.

Tynjala, Paivi, Jussi, Valimaa and Sarja, Anneli (2003), 'Pedagogical perspectives on the relationship between higher education and working life'. *Higher Education*, 46: 147–66.

UKCOSA (2006), *HE Statistics: How Many International Students are There in the UK?* Council for International Education. www. Ukcosa.org.uk/pages/hestats.htm.

Vaira, Massimiliano (2004), 'Globalization and higher education organization change: a framework for analysis'. *Higher Education*, 48: 483–510.

van der Wende, Marijk (2001), 'Internationalisation policies: about new trends and contrasting paradigms'. *Higher Education Policy*, 14: 249–59.

Vermunt, J.D. (2005), 'Relations between student learning patterns and personal and contextual factors and academic performance'. *Higher Education*, 49: 205–34.

Volet, S.E. (1999), 'Learning across cultures: appropriateness of knowledge transfer'. *International Journal of Educational Research*, 31(7): 625–43.

Volet, S. and Chalmers, D. (1997), 'Common misconceptions about students from South-East Asia studying in Australia', *Higher Education Research and Development*, 16: 87–98.

Volet, S.E., Renshaw, P.D. and Tietzel, K. (1994) 'A short-term longitudinal investigation of cross-cultural differences in study approaches using Biggs' SPQ questionnaire'. *British Journal of Educational Psychology*, 64: 301–18.

Wachter, Bernd (2003), 'An introduction: internationalisation at home in context'. *Journal of Studies in International Education*, 7(5): 5–11.

Waghid, Y. (2002), 'Knowledge productivity and higher education transformation in South Africa: towards reflexivity teaching, research and community services'. *Higher Education*, 43(4): 457–89.

Walker, Karen (2004), 'Teachers and teacher world-views'. *International Education Journal*, 5(3): 433–38.

Walker, P. (1999), 'Market research: a poor substitute for a scholarly investigation into international education issues in Britain'. *Journal of International Education*, 10(1): 6–13.

— (2001), 'Market or circus? Reflections on the commodification of British higher education from the international student experience'. *Education and Social Justice*, 3(2): 33–9.

Walters, David and Adams, Tony (2001), 'Global reach through a strategic operations approach: an Australian case study'. *Journal of Studies in International Education*, 5(4): 269–90.

Ward, C. (2001), 'The impact of international students on domestic students and host institutions'. Prepared for the Export Education Policy Project of the New Zealand Ministry of Education by Colleen Ward, Victoria University of Wellington. www.minedu.govt.nz.

Ward, C. and Masgoret, A.-M. (2004), *The Experiences of International Students in New Zealand: Report on the Results of the National Survey*. Prepared for the Ministry of Education by Ward, Colleen and Masgoret, Anne-Marie. Centre for Applied Cross-cultural Research and School of Psychology, Victoria University of Wellington, June.

Warhurst, Russell, P. (2006), '"We really felt part of something": participatory learning among peers within a university teaching-development community of practice'. *International Journal for Academic Development*, 11(2): 111–22.

Warren, D. (2005), 'Approaches to the challenge of student cultural diversity: learning from scholarship and practice', in Warren, D. and Fangarel, J. (eds), *Approaches to the Challenge of Student*

Cultural Diversity: Learning from scholarship and practice in International Conference on the Scholarship of Teaching and Learning. Proceedings 2003 and 2004, London: Education Development Centre, City University, 237–53.

Watson, David (2002), 'Can we do it all? Tensions in the mission and structure of UK higher education'. *Higher Education Quarterly*, 56(2): 143–55.

Webb, Graham (2005), 'Internationalisation of the curriculum: an institutional approach', in Carroll, Jude and Ryan, Janette (eds), *Teaching International Students: Improving Learning for All.* London: Routledge, 109–18.

Webb, M.S., Mayer, K.R., Pioche, V. and Allen, L.C. (1999), 'Internationalisation of American business education'. *Management International Review*, 39(4): 379–97.

Weert, Tom, Van, J. (2006), 'Education in the twenty-first century: new professionalism in lifelong learning, knowledge development and knowledge sharing'. *Education and Information Technologies*, 11(3–4): 217–37.

Welch, Anthony (2002), '"Going global" internationalizing Australian universities in a time of global crisis'. *Comparative Education Review*, 46(4): 433–71.

Wenger, E. (1998), *Communities of Practice: Learning, Meaning, and Identity.* Cambridge and New York: Cambridge University Press.

Whalley, T. (1997), *Best Practice Guidelines for Internationalizing the Curriculum.* Ministry of Education, Skills, and Training and the Centre for Curriculum, Transfer, and Technology, Province of British Columbia, Victoria, British Columbia, Canada.

— (2001), *Internationalizing Learning through Linked Assignments.* British Columbia Centre for International Education. www.bccie. bc.ca/bccie/FSA/Publications_Resources.asp#Preparing.

Wiers-Jenssen, J. (2002), 'Norwegian students abroad – experiences of students from Europe's northern boundary'. Paper presented at the 16th Australian International Education Conference, New Times, New Approaches, Hobart, Tasmania.

Williams, Gareth (1997), 'The market route to mass higher education: British experience 1979–1996'. *Higher Education Policy*, 10(3–4): 275–89.

Williams, K. (2005), 'Lecturer and first year student (mis)under-standings of assessment task verbs: "mind the gap". *Teaching in Higher Education*, 10(2): 157–73.

Wisker, G., Waller, S., Richter, U., Robinson, G., Trafford, V., Wicks, K. and Warnes, M. (2003), 'On nurturing hedgehogs: developments online for distance and offshore supervision'. surveys.canterbury.

ac.nz/herdsa03/pdfref/Y1199.pdf.

Wong, J. K. (2004), 'Are the learning styles of Asian internationals culturally or contextually based?' *International Education Journal,* 4(4): 154–66.

Woo, Henry, K.H. (1993), *The Making of a New Chinese Mind: Intellectuality and the Future of China.* Hong Kong: China Foundation.

Woodrow, Derek (2001), 'Cultural determinants of curricula, theories and practices'. *Pedagogy, Culture and Society,* 9(1): 5–27.

Woolf, Michael (2002), 'Harmony and dissonance in international education: the limits of globalisation'. *Journal of Studies in International Education,* 6(1): 5–15.

Wright, C. (1997), 'Gender matters: access, welfare, teaching and learning', in D. McNamara and R. Harris (eds) *Overseas Students in Higher Education: Issues in Teaching and Learning.* London and New York: Routledge, pp. 99–107.

Yan, Zhou (1998), 'Brain drain from Chinese universities in the 1990s'. *Journal of Contemporary China,* 7:17, 103–23.

Yang, Rui (2001), 'An Obstacle or a Useful Tool? The Role of the English Language in Internationalizing Chinese Universities'. *Journal of Studies in International Education,* 5(4): 341–58.

— (2002), 'University internationalization: its meanings, rationales and implications'. *Intercultural Education,* 13(1): 82–95.

Yershova, Y., DeJaegere, J. and Mestenhauser, J. (2000), 'Thinking not as usual: adding the intercultural perspective'. *Journal of Studies in International Education,* 4: 43–78.

Yielder, Jill and Codling, Andres (2004), 'Management and leadership in the contemporary university'. *Journal of Higher Education Policy and Management,* 26(3): 315–28.

Zepke, N. and Leach, L. (2005), 'Integration and adaptation: approaches to the student retention and achievement puzzle'. *Active Learning in Higher Education,* 6(1): 46–59.

Zhou, Y.R., Knoke, D. and Sakamoto, I. (2005), 'Rethinking silence in the classroom: Chinese students' experiences of sharing indigenous knowledge'. *International Journal of Inclusive Education,* 9(3): 287–311.

Zhu, Wei (2004), 'Writing in business courses: an analysis of assignment types, their characteristics and required skills'. *English for Specific Purposes,* 23: 111–35.

Zweig, David, Chen Changgui and Rosen, Stanley (2004), 'Globalization and transnational capital: overseas and returnee scholars to China'. *The China Quarterly,* 179: 735–57.

Index